The Book of Nature Myths

by Florence Holbrook

PREFACE.

In preparing the Book of Nature Myths the desire has been to make a second reader which would be adapted to the child's interest, ability, and progress.

The subject-matter is of permanent value, culled from the folk-lore of the primitive races; the vocabulary, based upon that of the Hiawatha Primer, is increased gradually, and the new words and phrases will add to the child's power of expression. The naive explanations of the phenomena of nature given by the primitive races appeal to the child's wonder about the same phenomena, and he is pleased and interested. These myths will gratify the child's desire for complete stories, and their intrinsic merit makes them valuable for oral reproduction.

The stories have been adapted to youthful minds from myths contained in the works of many students of folk-lore whose scholarship is undisputed. Special acknowledgment is due Miss Eva March Tappan for her valuable assistance in the final revision of the text.

CONTENTS.

THE BOOK OF NATURE MYTHS.

THE STORY OF THE FIRST HUMMING-BIRD.

PART I. THE GREAT FIRE-MOUNTAIN.

Long, long ago, when the earth was very young, two hunters were traveling through the forest. They had been on the track of a deer for many days, and they were now far away from the village where they lived. The sun went down and night came on. It was dark and gloomy, but over in the western sky there came a bright light.

"It is the moon," said one.

"No," said the other. "We have watched many and many a night to see the great, round moon rise above the trees. That is not the moon. Is it the northern lights?"

"No, the northern lights are not like this, and it is not a comet. What can it be?"

It is no wonder that the hunters were afraid, for the flames flared red over the sky like a wigwam on fire. Thick, blue smoke floated above the flames and hid the shining stars.

"Do the flames and smoke come from the wigwam of the Great Spirit?" asked one.

"I fear that he is angry with his children, and that the flames are his fiery war-clubs," whispered the other. No sleep came to their eyes. All night long they watched and wondered, and waited in terror for the morning.

When morning came, the two hunters were still watching the sky. Little by little they saw that there was a high mountain in the west where the light had been, and above the mountain floated a dark blue smoke. "Come," said one, "we will go and see what it is."

They walked and walked till they came close to the mountain, and then they saw fire shining through the seams of the rocks. "It is a mountain of fire," one whispered. "Shall we go on?" "We will," said the other, and they went higher and higher up the mountain. At last they stood upon its highest point. "Now we know the secret," they cried. "Our people will be glad when they hear this."

Swiftly they went home through the forest to their own village. "We have found a wonder," they cried. "We have found the home of the Fire Spirit. We know where she keeps her flames to help the Great Spirit and his children. It is a mountain of fire. Blue smoke rises above it night and day, for its heart is a fiery sea, and on the sea the red flames leap and dance. Come with us to the wonderful mountain of fire."

The people of the village had been cold in the winter nights, and they cried, "O brothers, your words are good. We will move our lodges to the foot of the magic mountain. We can light our wigwam fires from its flames, and we shall not fear that we shall perish in the long, cold nights of winter."

So the Indians went to live at the foot of the fire-mountain, and when the cold nights came, they said, "We are not cold, for the Spirit of Fire is our good friend, and she keeps her people from perishing."

PART II. THE FROLIC OF THE FLAMES.

For many and many a moon the people of the village lived at the foot of the great fire-mountain. On summer evenings, the children watched the light, and when a child asked, "Father, what makes it?" the father said, "That is the home of the Great Spirit of Fire, who is our good friend." Then all in the little village went to sleep and lay safely on their beds till the coming of the morning.

But one night when all the people in the village were asleep, the flames in the mountain had a great frolic. They danced upon the sea of fire as warriors dance the war-dance. They seized great rocks and threw them at the sky. The smoke above them hid the stars; the mountain throbbed and trembled. Higher and still higher sprang the dancing flames. At last, they leaped clear above the highest point of the mountain and started down it in a river of red fire. Then the gentle Spirit of Fire called, "Come back, my flames, come back again! The people in the village will not know that you are in a frolic, and they will be afraid."

The flames did not heed her words, and the river of fire ran on and on, straight down the mountain. The flowers in its pathway perished. It leaped upon great trees and bore them to the earth. It drove the birds from their nests, and they fluttered about in the thick smoke. It hunted the wild creatures of the forest from the thickets where they hid, and they fled before it in terror.

At last, one of the warriors in the village awoke. The thick smoke was in his nostrils. In his ears was the war-cry of the flames. He sprang to the door of his lodge and saw the fiery river leaping down the mountain. "My people, my people," he cried, "the flames are upon us!" With cries of fear the people in the village fled far away into the forest, and the flames feasted upon the homes they loved.

The two hunters went to look upon the mountain, and when they came back, they said sadly, "There are no flowers on the mountain. Not a bird-song did we hear. Not a living creature did we see. It is all dark and gloomy. We know the fire is there, for the blue smoke still floats up to the sky, but the mountain will never again be our friend."

PART III. THE BIRD OF FLAME

When the Great Spirit saw the work of the flames, he was very angry. "The fires of this mountain must perish," he said. "No longer shall its red flames light the midnight sky."

The mountain trembled with fear at the angry words of the Great Spirit. "O father of all fire and light," cried the Fire Spirit, "I know that the flames have been cruel. They killed the beautiful flowers and drove your children from their homes, but for many, many moons they heeded my words and were good and gentle. They drove the frost and cold of winter from the wigwams of the village. The little children laughed to see their red light in the sky. The hearts of your people will be sad, if the flames must perish from the earth."

The Great Spirit listened to the words of the gentle Spirit of Fire, but he answered, "The fires must perish. They have been cruel to my people, and the little children will fear them now; but because the children once loved them, the beautiful colors of the flames shall still live to make glad the hearts of all who look upon them."

Then the Great Spirit struck the mountain with his magic war-club. The smoke above it faded away; its fires grew cold and dead. In its dark and gloomy heart only one little flame still trembled. It looked like a star. How beautiful it was!

The Great Spirit looked upon the little flame. He saw that it was beautiful and gentle, and he loved it. "The fires of the mountain must perish," he said, "but you little, gentle flame, shall have wings and fly far away from the cruel fires, and all my children will love you as I do." Swiftly the little thing rose above the mountain and flew away in the sunshine. The light of the flames was still on its head; their marvelous colors were on its wings.

So from the mountain's heart of fire sprang the first humming-bird. It is the bird of flame, for it has all the beauty of the colors of the flame, but it is gentle, and every child in all the earth loves it and is glad to see it fluttering over the flowers.

THE STORY OF THE FIRST BUTTERFLIES.

The Great Spirit thought, "By and by I will make men, but first I will make a home for them. It shall be very bright and beautiful. There shall be mountains and prairies and forests, and about it all shall be the blue waters of the sea."

As the Great Spirit had thought, so he did. He gave the earth a soft cloak of green. He made the prairies beautiful with flowers. The forests were bright with birds of many colors, and the sea was the home of wonderful sea-creatures. "My children will love the prairies, the forests, and the seas," he thought, "but the mountains look dark and cold. They are very dear to me, but how shall I make my children go to them and so learn to love them?"

Long the Great Spirit thought about the mountains. At last, he made many little shining stones. Some were red, some blue, some green, some yellow, and some were shining with all the lovely colors of the beautiful rainbow. "All my children will love what is beautiful," he thought, "and if I hide the bright stones in the seams of the rocks of the mountains, men will come to find them, and they will learn to love my mountains."

When the stones were made and the Great Spirit looked upon their beauty, he said, "I will not hide you all away in the seams of the rocks. Some of you shall be out in the sunshine, so that the little children who cannot go to the mountains shall see your colors." Then the southwind came by, and as he went, he sang softly of forests flecked with light and shadow, of birds and their nests in the leafy trees. He sang of long summer days and the music of waters beating upon the shore. He sang of the moonlight and the starlight. All the wonders of the night, all the beauty of the morning, were in his song.

"Dear southwind," said the Great Spirit "here are some beautiful things for you to bear away with, you to your summer home. You will love them, and all the little children will love them." At these words of the Great Spirit, all the stones before him stirred with life and lifted themselves on many-colored wings. They fluttered away in the sunshine, and the southwind sang to them as they went.

So it was that the first butterflies came from a beautiful thought of the Great

Spirit, and in their wings were all the colors of the shining stones that he did not wish to hide away.

HE STORY OF THE FIRST WOODPECKER.

In the days of long ago the Great Spirit came down from the sky and talked with men. Once as he went up and down the earth, he came to the wigwam of a woman. He went into the wigwam and sat down by the fire, but he looked like an old man, and the woman did not know who he was.

"I have fasted for many days," said the Great Spirit to the woman. "Will you give me some food?" The woman made a very little cake and put it on the fire. "You can have this cake," she said, "if you will wait for it to bake." "I will wait," he said.

When the cake was baked, the woman stood and looked at it. She thought, "It is very large. I thought it was small. I will not give him so large a cake as that." So she put it away and made a small one. "If you will wait, I will give you this when it is baked," she said, and the Great Spirit said, "I will wait."

When that cake was baked, it was larger than the first one. "It is so large that I will keep it for a feast," she thought. So she said to her guest, "I will not give you this cake, but if you will wait, I will make you another one." "I will wait," said the Great Spirit again.

Then the woman made another cake. It was still smaller than the others had been at first, but when she went to the fire for it, she found it the largest of all. She did not know that the Great Spirit's magic had made each cake larger, and she thought, "This is a marvel, but I will not give away the largest cake of all." So she said to her guest, "I have no food for you. Go to the forest and look there for your food. You can find it in the bark of the trees, if you will."

The Great Spirit was angry when he heard the words of the woman. He rose up from where he sat and threw back his cloak. "A woman must be good and gentle," he said, "and you are cruel. You shall no longer be a woman and live in a wigwam. You shall go out into the forest and hunt for your food in the bark of trees."

The Great Spirit stamped his foot on the earth, and the woman grew smaller and smaller. Wings started from her body and feathers grew upon her. With a loud cry she rose from the earth and flew away to the forest.

And to this day all woodpeckers live in the forest and hunt for their food in the bark of trees.

WHY THE WOODPECKER'S HEAD IS RED.

One day the woodpecker said to the Great Spirit, "Men do not like me. I wish they did."

The Great Spirit said, "If you wish men to love you, you must be good to them and help them. Then they will call you their friend."

"How can a little bird help a man?" asked the woodpecker.

"If one wishes to help, the day will come when he can help," said the Great Spirit. The day did come, and this story shows how a little bird helped a strong warrior.

There was once a cruel magician who lived in a gloomy wigwam beside the Black-Sea-Water. He did not like flowers, and they did not blossom in his pathway. He did not like birds, and they did not sing in the trees above him. The breath of his nostrils was fatal to all life. North, south, east, and west he blew the deadly fever that killed the women and the little children.

"Can I help them?" thought a brave warrior, and he said, "I will find the magician, and see if death will not come to him as he has made it come to others. I will go straightway to his home."

For many days the brave warrior was in his canoe traveling across the Black-Sea-Water. At last he saw the gloomy wigwam of the cruel magician. He shot an arrow at the door and called, "Come out, O coward! You have killed women and children with your fatal breath, but you cannot kill a warrior. Come out and fight, if you are not afraid."

The cruel magician laughed loud and long. "One breath of fever," he said, "and you will fall to the earth." The warrior shot again, and then the magician was angry. He did not laugh, but he came straight out of his gloomy lodge, and as he came, he blew the fever all about him.

Then was seen the greatest fight that the sun had ever looked upon. The brave warrior shot his flint-tipped arrows, but the magician had on his magic cloak, and the arrows could not wound him. He blew from his nostrils the deadly breath of fever, but the heart of the warrior was so strong that the fever could not kill him.

At last the brave warrior had but three arrows in his quiver. "What shall I do?" he said sadly. "My arrows are good and my aim is good, but no arrow can go through the magic cloak."

"Come on, come on," called the magician. "You are the man who wished to fight. Come on." Then a woodpecker in a tree above the brave warrior said softly, "Aim your arrow at his head, O warrior! Do not shoot at his heart, but at the crest of feathers on his head. He can be wounded there, but not in his heart."

The warrior was not so proud that he could not listen to a little bird. The magician bent to lift a stone, and an arrow flew from the warrior's bow. It buzzed and stung like a wasp. It came so close to the crest of feathers that the magician trembled with terror. Before he could run, another arrow came, and this one struck him right on his crest. His heart grew cold with fear. "Death has struck me," he cried.

"Your cruel life is over," said the warrior. "People shall no longer fear your fatal breath." Then he said to the woodpecker, "Little bird, you have been a good friend to me, and I will do all that I can for you." He put some of the red blood of the magician upon the little creature's head. It made the crest of feathers there as red as flame. "Whenever a man looks upon you," said the warrior, "he will say, 'That bird is our friend. He helped to kill the cruel magician.'"

The little woodpecker was very proud of his red crest because it showed that he was the friend of man, and all his children to this day are as proud as he was.

WHY THE CAT ALWAYS FALLS UPON HER FEET.

Some magicians are cruel, but others are gentle and good to all the creatures of the earth. One of these good magicians was one day traveling in a great forest. The sun rose high in the heavens, and he lay down at the foot of a tree. Soft, green moss grew all about him. The sun shining through the leaves made flecks of light and shadow upon the earth. He heard the song of the bird and the lazy buzz of the wasp. The wind rustled the leafy boughs above him. All the music of the forest lulled him to slumber, and he closed his eyes.

As the magician lay asleep, a great serpent came softly from the thicket. It lifted high its shining crest and saw the man at the foot of the tree. "I will kill him!" it hissed. "I could have eaten that cat last night if he had not called, 'Watch, little cat, watch!' I will kill him, I will kill him!"

Closer and closer the deadly serpent moved. The magician stirred in his sleep. "Watch, little cat, watch!" he said softly. The serpent drew back, but the magician's eyes were shut, and it went closer. It hissed its war-cry. The sleeping magician did not move. The serpent was upon him--no, far up in the high branches of the tree above his head the little cat lay hidden. She had seen the serpent when it came from the thicket.

She watched it as it went closer and closer to the sleeping man, and she heard it hiss its war-cry. The little cat's body quivered with anger and with fear, for she was so little and the serpent was so big. "The magician was very good to me," she thought, and she leaped down upon the serpent.

Oh, how angry the serpent was! It hissed, and the flames shot from its eyes. It struck wildly at the brave little cat, but now the cat had no fear. Again and again she leaped upon the serpent's head, and at last the creature lay dead beside the sleeping man whom it had wished to kill.

When the magician awoke, the little cat lay on the earth, and not far away was the dead serpent. He knew at once what the cat had done, and he said, "Little cat, what can I do to show you honor for your brave fight? Your eyes are quick to see, and your ears are quick to hear. You can run very swiftly. I know what I can do for you. You shall be known over the earth as the friend of man, and you shall always have a home in the home of man. And one thing more, little cat: you leaped from the high tree to kill the deadly serpent, and now as long as you live, you shall leap where you will, and you shall always fall upon your feet."

WHY THE SWALLOW'S TAIL IS FORKED.

This is the story of how the swallow's tail came to be forked.

One day the Great Spirit asked all the animals that he had made to come to his lodge. Those that could fly came first: the robin, the bluebird, the owl, the butterfly, the wasp, and the firefly. Behind them came the chicken, fluttering its wings and trying hard to keep up. Then came the deer, the squirrel, the serpent, the cat, and the rabbit. Last of all came the bear, the beaver, and the hedgehog. Every one traveled as swiftly as he could, for each wished to hear the words of the Great Spirit.

"I have called you together," said the Great Spirit, "because I often hear you scold and fret. What do you wish me to do for you? How can I help you?"

"I do not like to hunt so long for my food," said the bear.

"I do not like to build nests," said the bluebird.

"I do not like to live in the water," said the beaver.

"And I do not like to live in a tree," said the squirrel.

At last man stood erect before the Great Spirit and said, "O Great Father, the serpent feasts upon my blood. Will you not give him some other food?"

"And why?" asked the Great Spirit.

"Because I am the first of all the creatures you have made," answered man proudly.

Then every animal in the lodge was angry to hear the words of man. The squirrel chattered, the wasp buzzed, the owl hooted, and the serpent hissed.

"Hush, be still," said the Great Spirit. "You are, O man, the first of my creatures, but I am the father of all. Each one has his rights, and the serpent must have his food. Mosquito, you are a great traveler. Now fly away and find what creature's blood is best for the serpent. Do you all come back in a year and a day."

The animals straightway went to their homes. Some went to the river, some to the forest, and some to the prairie, to wait for the day when they must meet at the lodge of the Great Spirit.

The mosquito traveled over the earth and stung every creature that he met to find whose blood was the best for the serpent. On his way back to the lodge of the Great Spirit he looked up into the sky, and there was the swallow.

"Good-day, swallow," called the mosquito.

"I am glad to see you, my friend," sang the swallow. "Are you going to the lodge of the Great Spirit? And have you found out whose blood is best for the serpent?"

"The blood of man," answered the mosquito.

The mosquito did not like man, but the swallow had always been his friend. "What can I do to help man?" he thought. "Oh, I know what I can do." Then he asked the mosquito, "Whose blood did you say?"

"Man's blood," said the mosquito; "that is best."

"This is best," said the swallow, and he tore out the mosquito's tongue.

The mosquito buzzed angrily and went quickly to the Great Spirit.

"All the animals are here," said the Great Spirit. "They are waiting to hear whose blood is best for the serpent."

The mosquito tried to answer, "The blood of man," but he could not say a word. He could make no sound but "Kss-ksss-ksssss!"

"What do you say?"

"Kss-ksss-ksssss!" buzzed the mosquito angrily.

All the creatures wondered. Then said the swallow:--

"Great Father, the mosquito is timid and cannot answer you. I met him before we came, and he told me whose blood it was."

"Then let us know at once," said the Great Spirit.

"It is the blood of the frog," answered the swallow quickly. "Is it not so, friend mosquito?"

"Kss-ksss-ksssss!" hissed the angry mosquito.

"The serpent shall have the frog's blood," said the Great Spirit. "Man shall be his food no longer."

Now the serpent was angry with the swallow, for he did not like frog's blood. As the swallow flew near him, he seized him by the tail and tore away a little of it. This is why the swallow's tail is forked, and it is why man always looks upon the swallow as his friend.

WHY THE WHITE HARES HAVE BLACK EARS.

In the forest there is a beautiful spirit. All the beasts and all the birds are dear to him, and he likes to have them gentle and good. One morning he saw some of his little white hares fighting one another, and each trying to seize the best of the food.

"Oh, my selfish little hares," he said sadly, "why do you fight and try to seize the best of everything for yourselves? Why do you not live in love together?"

"Tell us a story and we will be good," cried the hares.

Then the spirit of the forest was glad. "I will tell you a story of how you first came to live on the green earth with the other animals," he said, "and why it is that you are white, and the other hares are not."

Then the little hares came close about the spirit of the forest, and sat very still to hear the story.

"Away up above the stars," the gentle spirit began, "the sky children were all together one snowy day. They threw snowflakes at one another, and some of the snowflakes fell from the sky. They came down swiftly between the stars and among the branches of the trees. At last they lay on the green earth. They were the first that had ever come to the earth, and no one knew what they were. The swallow asked, 'What are they?' and the butterfly answered, 'I do not know.' The spirit of the sky was listening, and he said, 'We call them snowflakes.'

"'I never heard of snowflakes. Are they birds or beasts?' asked the butterfly.

"'They are snowflakes,' answered the spirit of the sky, 'but they are magic snowflakes. Watch them closely.'

"The swallow and the butterfly watched. Every snowflake showed two bright eyes, then two long ears, then some soft feet, and there were the whitest, softest little hares that were ever seen."

"Were we the little white hares?" asked the listeners.

"You were the little white hares," answered the spirit, "and if you are gentle and good, you will always be white."

The hares were not gentle and good; they were fretful, and before long they were scolding and fighting again. The gentle spirit was angry. "I must get a firebrand and beat them with it," he said, "for they must learn to be good."

So the hares were beaten with the firebrand till their ears were black as night. Their bodies were still white, but if the spirit hears them scolding and fighting again, it may be that we shall see their bodies as black as their ears.

WHY THE MAGPIE'S NEST IS NOT WELL BUILT.

A long time ago all the birds met together to talk about building nests.

"Every Indian has a wigwam," said the robin, "and every bird needs a home."

"Indians have no feathers," said the owl, "and so they are cold without wigwams. We have feathers."

"I keep warm by flying swiftly," said the swallow.

"And I keep warm by fluttering my wings," said the humming-bird.

"By and by we shall have our little ones," said the robin. "They will have no feathers on their wings, so they cannot fly or flutter; and they will be cold. How shall we keep them warm if we have no nests?"

Then all the birds said, "We will build nests so that our little ones will be warm."

The birds went to work. One brought twigs, one brought moss, and one brought leaves. They sang together merrily, for they thought of the little ones that would some time come to live in the warm nests.

Now the magpie was lazy, and she sat still and watched the others at their work.

"Come and build your nest in the reeds and rushes," cried one bird, but the magpie said "No."

"My nest is on the branch of a tree," called another, "and it rocks like a child's cradle. Come and build beside it," but the magpie said "No."

Before long all the birds but the magpie had their nests built. The magpie cried, "I do not know how to build a nest. Will you not help me?"

The other birds were sorry for her and answered, "We will teach you." The black-bird said, "Put the twigs on this bough;" the robin said, "Put the leaves between the twigs;" and the humming-bird said, "Put this soft green moss over it all."

"I do not know how," cried the magpie.

"We are teaching you," said the other birds. But the magpie was lazy, and she thought, "If I do not learn, they will build a nest for me."

The other birds talked together. "She does not wish to learn," they said, "and we will not help her any longer." So they went away from her.

Then the magpie was sorry. "Come back," she called, "and I will learn." But by this time the other birds had eggs in their nests, and they were busy taking care of them, and had no time to teach the lazy magpie. This is why the magpie's nest is not well built.

WHY THE RAVEN'S FEATHERS ARE BLACK.

Long, long ago the raven's feathers were white as snow. He was a beautiful bird, but the other birds did not like him because he was a thief. When they saw him coming, they would hide away the things that they cared for most, but in some marvelous way he always found them and took them to his nest in the pine-tree.

One morning the raven heard a little bird singing merrily in a thicket. The leaves of the trees were dark green, and the little bird's yellow feathers looked like sunshine among them.

"I will have that bird," said the raven, and he seized the trembling little thing.

The yellow bird fluttered and cried, "Help, help! Will no one come and help me!"

The other birds happened to be far away, and not one heard her cries. "The raven will kill me," she called. "Help, help!"

Now hidden in the bark of a tree was a wood-worm.

"I am only a wood-worm," he said to himself, "and I cannot fly like a bird, but the yellow bird has been good to me, and I will do what I can to help her."

When the sun set, the raven went to sleep. Then the wood-worm made his way softly up the pine-tree to the raven's nest, and bound his feet together with grass and pieces of birch-bark.

"Fly away," whispered the wood-worm softly to the little yellow bird, "and come to see me by and by. I must teach the raven not to be cruel to the other birds."

The little yellow bird flew away, and the wood-worm brought twigs, and moss, and birch-bark, and grass, and put them around the tree. Then he set them all on fire. Up the great pine-tree went the flames, leaping from bough to bough.

"Fire! fire!" cried the raven. "Come and help me! My nest is on fire!"

The other birds were not sorry to see him flutter. "He is a thief," said they. "Let him be in the fire."

By and by the fire burned the grass and the pieces of birch-bark that fastened his feet together, and the raven flew away. He was not burned, but he could no longer be proud of his shining white feathers, for the smoke had made every one of them as black as night.

HOW FIRE WAS BROUGHT TO THE INDIANS.

PART I. SEIZING THE FIREBRAND.

Oh, it was so cold! The wind blew the leaves about on the ground. The frost spirit hid on the north side of every tree, and stung every animal of the forest that came near. Then the snow fell till the ground was white. Through the snowflakes one could see the sun, but the sun looked cold, for it was not a clear, bright yellow. It was almost as white as the moon.

The Indians drew their cloaks more and more closely around them, for they had no fire.

"How shall we get fire?" they asked, but no one answered.

All the fire on earth was in the wigwam of two old women who did not like the Indians.

"They shall not have it," said the old women, and they watched night and day so that no one could get a firebrand.

At last a young Indian said to the others, "No man can get fire. Let us ask the animals to help us."

"What beast or what bird can get fire when the two old women are watching it?" the others cried.

"The bear might get it."

"No, he cannot run swiftly."

"The deer can run."

"His antlers would not go through the door of the wigwam."

"The raven can go through the door."

"It was smoke that made the raven's feathers black, and now he always keeps away from the fire."

"The serpent has not been in the smoke."

"No, but he is not our friend, and he will not do anything for us."

"Then I will ask the wolf," said the young man. "He can run, he has no antlers, and he has not been in the smoke."

So the young man went to the wolf and called, "Friend wolf, if you will get us a firebrand, I will give you some food every day."

"I will get it," said the wolf. "Go to the home of the old women and hide behind a tree; and when you hear me cough three times, give a loud war-cry."

Close by the village of the Indians was a pond. In the pond was a frog, and near the pond lived a squirrel, a bat, a bear, and a deer. The wolf cried, "Frog, hide in the rushes across the pond. Squirrel, go to the bushes beside the path that runs from the pond to the wigwam of the two old women. Bat, go into the shadow and sleep if you like, but do not close both eyes. Bear, do not stir from behind this great rock till you are told. Deer, keep still as a mountain till something happens."

The wolf then went to the wigwam of the two old women. He coughed at the door, and at last they said, "Wolf, you may come in to the fire."

The wolf went into the wigwam. He coughed three times, and the Indian gave a war-cry. The two old women ran out quickly into the forest to see what had happened, and the wolf ran away with a firebrand from the fire.

PART II. THE FIREBRAND IN THE FOREST.

When the two women saw that the wolf had the firebrand, they were very angry, and straightway they ran after him.

"Catch it and run!" cried the wolf, and he threw it to the deer. The deer caught it and ran.

"Catch it and run!" cried the deer, and he threw it to the bear. The bear caught it and ran.

"Catch it and fly!" cried the bear, and he threw it to the bat. The bat caught it and flew.

"Catch it and run!" cried the bat, and he threw it to the squirrel. The squirrel caught it and ran.

"Oh, serpent," called the two old women, "you are no friend to the Indians. Help us. Get the firebrand away from the squirrel."

As the squirrel ran swiftly over the ground, the serpent sprang up and tried to seize the firebrand. He did not get it, but the smoke went into the squirrel's nostrils and made him cough. He would not let go of the firebrand, but ran and ran till he could throw it to the frog.

When the frog was running away with it, then the squirrel for the first time thought of himself, and he found that his beautiful bushy tail was no longer straight, for the fire had curled it up over his back.

"Do not be sorry," called the young Indian across the pond. "Whenever an Indian boy sees a squirrel with his tail curled up over his back, he will throw him a nut."

PART III. THE FIREBRAND IN THE POND.

All this time the firebrand was burning, and the frog was going to the pond as fast as he could. The old women were running after him, and when he came to the water, one of them caught him by the tail.

"I have caught him!" she called.

"Do not let him go!" cried the other.

"No, I will not," said the first; but she did let him go, for the little frog tore himself away and dived into the water. His tail was still in the woman's hand, but the firebrand was safe, and he made his way swiftly across the pond.

"Here it is," said the frog.

"Where?" asked the young Indian. Then the frog coughed, and out of his mouth came the firebrand. It was small, for it had been burning all this time, but it set fire to the leaves and twigs, and soon the Indians were warm again. They sang and they danced about the flames.

At first the frog was sad, because he was sorry to lose his tail; but before long he was as merry as the people who were dancing, for the young Indian said, "Little frog, you have been a good friend to us, and as long as we live on the earth, we will never throw a stone at a frog that has no tail."

HOW THE QUAIL BECAME A SNIPE.

"It is lonely living in this great tree far away from the other birds," said the owl to herself. "I will get some one to come and live with me. The quail has many children, and I will ask her for one of them."

The owl went to the quail and said, "Will you let me have one of your children to come and live with me?"

"Live with you? No," answered the quail. "I would as soon let my child live with the serpent. You are hidden in the tree all day long, and when it is dark, you come down like a thief and catch little animals that are fast asleep in their nests. You shall never have one of my children."

"I will have one," thought the owl.

She waited till the night had come. It was dark and gloomy, for the moon was not to be seen, and not a star twinkled in the sky. Not a leaf stirred, and not a ripple was on the pond. The owl crept up to the quail's home as softly as she could. The young birds were chattering together, and she listened to their talk.

"My mother is gone a long time," said one. "It is lonely, and I am afraid."

"What is there to be afraid of?" asked another. "You are a little coward. Shut your eyes and go to sleep. See me! I am not afraid, if it is dark and gloomy. Oh, oh!" cried the boaster, for the owl had seized him and was carrying him away from home and his little brothers.

When the mother quail came home, she asked, "Where is your brother?" The little quails did not know. All they could say was that something had seized him in the darkness and taken him away.

"It crept up to the nest in the dark," said one.

"And oh, mother, never, never go away from us again!" cried another. "Do not leave us at home all alone."

"But, my dear little ones," the mother said, "how could you have any food if I never went away from our home?"

The mother quail was very sad, and she would have been still more sorrowful if she had known what was happening to her little son far away in the owl's nest. The cruel owl had pulled and pulled on the quail's bill and legs, till they were so long that his mother would not have known him.

One night the mole came to the quail and said, "Your little son is in the owl's nest."

"How do you know?" asked the quail.

"I cannot see very well," answered the mole, "but I heard him call, and I know that he is there."

"How shall I get him away from the owl?" the quail asked the mole.

"The owl crept up to your home in the dark," said the mole, "but you must go to her nest at sunrise when the light shines in her eyes and she cannot see you."

At sunrise the quail crept up to the owl's nest and carried away her dear little son to his old home. As the light grew brighter, she saw what had happened to him. His bill and his legs were so long that he did not look like her son.

"He is not like our brother," said the other little quails.

"That is because the cruel owl that carried him away has pulled his bill and his legs," answered the mother sorrowfully. "You must be very good to him."

But the other little quails were not good to him. They laughed at him, and the quail with the long bill and legs was never again merry and glad with them. Before long he ran away and hid among the great reeds that stand in the water and on the shores of the pond.

"I will not be called quail," he said to himself, "for quails never have long bills and legs. I will have a new name, and it shall be snipe. I like the sound of that name."

So it was that the bird whose name was once quail came to be called snipe. His children live among the reeds of the pond, and they, too, are called snipes.

WHY THE SERPENT SHEDS HIS SKIN.

The serpent is the grandfather of the owl, and once upon a time if the owl needed help, she would say, "My grandfather will come and help me," but now he never comes to her. This story tells why.

When the owl carried away the little quail, she went to the serpent and said, "Grandfather, you will not tell the quail that I have her son, will you?"

"No," answered the serpent, "I will keep your secret. I will not whisper it to any one." So when the mother quail asked all the animals, "Can you tell me who has carried away my little son?" the serpent answered, "I have been sound asleep. How could I know?"

After the quail had become a snipe and had gone to live in the marsh among the reeds, the cruel owl looked everywhere for him, and at last she saw him standing beside a great stone in the water.

She went to the serpent and said, "Grandfather, will you do something for me?"

"I will," hissed the serpent softly, "What is it?"

"Only to take a drink of water," answered the owl. "Come and drink all the water in the marsh, and then I can catch the quail that I made into a snipe."

The serpent drank and drank, but still there was water in the marsh.

"Why do you not drink faster?" cried the owl. "I shall never get the snipe."

The serpent drank till he could drink no more, and still the water stood in the marsh. The owl could not see well by day, and the serpent could not see above the reeds and rushes, so they did not know that the water from the pond was coming into the marsh faster than the serpent could drink it.

Still the serpent drank, and at last his skin burst.

"Oh," he cried, "my skin has burst. Help me to fasten it together."

"My skin never bursts," said the owl. "If you will drink the water from the marsh, I will help you, but I will not fasten any skin together till I get that snipe."

The serpent had done all that he could to help the owl, and now he was angry. He was afraid, too, for he did not know what would happen to him, and he lay on the ground trembling and quivering. It was not long before his old skin fell off, and then he saw that under it was a beautiful new one, all bright and shining. He sheds his old skin every year now, but never again has he done anything to help the owl.

WHY THE DOVE IS TIMID.

A spirit called the manito always watches over the Indians. He is glad when they are brave, but if they are cowardly, he is angry.

One day when the manito was walking under the pine-trees, he heard a cry of terror in the forest.

"What is that?" said he. "Can it be that any of my Indian children are afraid?"

As he stood listening, an Indian boy came running from the thicket, crying in fear.

"What are you afraid of?" asked the manito.

"My mother told me to go into the forest with my bow and arrows and shoot some animal for food," said the boy.

"That is what all Indian boys must do," said the manito. "Why do you not do as she said?"

"Oh, the great bear is in the forest, and I am afraid of him!"

"Afraid of Hoots?" asked the manito. "An Indian boy must never be afraid."

"But Hoots will eat me, I know he will," cried the boy. "Boo-hoo, boo-hoo!"

"A boy must be brave," said the manito, "and I will not have a coward among my Indians. You are too timid ever to be a warrior, and so you shall be a bird. Whenever Indian boys look at you, they will say, 'There is the boy who was afraid of Hoots.'"

The boy's cloak of deerskin fell off, and feathers came out all over his body. His feet were no longer like a boy's feet, they were like the feet of a bird. His bow and arrows fell upon the grass, for he had no longer any hands with which to hold them. He tried to call to his mother, but the only sound he could make was "Hoo, hoo!"

"Now you are a dove," said the manito, "and a dove you shall be as long as you live. You shall always be known as the most timid of birds."

Again the dove that had once been a boy tried to call, but he only said, "Hoo, hoo!"

"That is the only sound you will ever make," said the manito, "and when the other boys hear it, they will say, 'Listen! He was afraid of Hoots, the bear, and that is why he says Hoo, hoo!'"

WHY THE PARROT REPEATS THE WORDS OF MEN.

In the olden times when the earth was young, all the birds knew the language of men and could talk with them. Everybody liked the parrot, because he always told things as they were, and they called him the bird that tells the truth.

This bird that always told the truth lived with a man who was a thief, and one night the man killed another man's ox and hid its flesh.

When the other man came to look for it in the morning, he asked the thief, "Have you seen my ox?"

"No, I have not seen it," said the man.

"Is that the truth?" the owner asked.

"Yes, it is. I have not seen the ox," repeated the man.

"Ask the parrot," said one of the villagers. "He always tells the truth."

"O bird of truth," said they to the parrot, "did this man kill an ox and hide its flesh?"

"Yes, he did," answered the parrot.

The thief knew well that the villagers would punish him the next day, if he could not make them think that the parrot did not always tell the truth.

"I have it," he said to himself at last. "I know what I can do."

When night came he put a great jar over the parrot. Then he poured water upon the jar and struck it many times with a tough piece of oak. This he did half the night. Then he went to bed and was soon fast asleep.

In the morning the men came to punish him.

"How do you know that I killed the ox?" he asked.

"Because the bird of truth says that you did," they answered.

"The bird of truth!" he cried. "That parrot is no bird of truth. He will not tell the truth even about what happened last night. Ask him if the moon was shining."

"Did the moon shine last night?" the men asked.

"No," answered the parrot. "There was no moon, for the rain fell, and there was a great storm in the heavens. I heard the thunder half the night."

"This bird has always told the truth before," said the villagers, "but there was no storm last night and the moon was bright. What shall we do to punish the parrot?" they asked the thief.

"I think we will no longer let him live in our homes," answered the thief.

"Yes," said the others, "he must fly away to the forest, and even when there is a storm, he can no longer come to our homes, because we know now that he is a bird of a lying tongue."

So the parrot flew away sorrowfully into the lonely forest. He met a mocking-bird and told him what had happened.

"Why did you not repeat men's words as I do?" asked the mocking-bird. "Men always think their own words are good."

"But the man's words were not true," said the parrot.

"That is nothing," replied the mocking-bird, laughing. "Say what they say, and they will think you are a wonderful bird."

"Yes, I see," said the parrot thoughtfully, "and I will never again be punished for telling the truth. I will only repeat the words of others."

THE STORY OF THE FIRST MOCKING-BIRD.

Far away in the forest there once lived the most cruel man on all the earth. He did not like the Indians, and he said to himself, "Some day I will be ruler of them all." Then he thought, "There are many brave warriors among the Indians, and I must first put them to death."

He was cunning as well as cruel, and he soon found a way to kill the warriors. He built some wigwams and made fires before them as if people lived in each one.

One day a hunter on his way home heard a baby crying in one of the wigwams. He went in, but he never came out again. Another day a hunter heard a child laughing. He went in, but he never came out again. So it was day after day. One hunter heard a woman talking, and went to see who it was; another heard a man calling to people in the other wigwams, and went to see who they were; and no one who once went into a wigwam ever came out.

One young brave had heard the voices, but he feared there was magic about them, and so he had never gone into the wigwams; but when he saw that his friends did not come back, he went to the wigwams and called, "Where are all the people that I have heard talk and laugh?"

"Talk and laugh," said the cunning man mockingly.

"Where are they? Do you know?" cried the brave, and the cunning man called, "Do you know?" and laughed.

"Whose voices have I heard?"

"Have I heard?" mocked the cunning man.

"I heard a baby cry."

"Cry," said the cunning man.

"Who is with you?"

"You."

Then the young brave was angry. He ran into the first wigwam, and there he found the man who had cried like a baby and talked in a voice like a woman's and made all the other sounds. The brave caught him by the leg and threw him down upon the earth.

"It was you who cried and talked and laughed," he said. "I heard your voice and now you are going to be punished for killing our braves. Where is my brother, and where are our friends?"

"How do I know?" cried the man. "Ask the sun or the moon or the fire if you will, but do not ask me;" and all the time he was trying to pull the young brave into the flames.

"I will ask the fire," said the brave. "Fire, you are a good friend to us Indians. What has this cruel man done with our warriors?"

The fire had no voice, so it could not answer, but it sprang as far away from the hunter as it could, and there where the flames had been he saw two stone arrowheads.

"I know who owned the two arrowheads," said the brave. "You have thrown my friends into your fire. Now I will do to you what you have done to them."

He threw the cunning man into the fire. His head burst into two pieces, and from between them a bird flew forth. Its voice was loud and clear, but it had no song of its own. It could only mock the songs of other birds, and that is why it is called the mocking-bird.

WHY THE TAIL OF THE FOX HAS A WHITE TIP.

"I must have a boy to watch my sheep and my cows," thought an old woman, and so she went out to look for a boy. She looked first in the fields and then in the forest, but nowhere could she find a boy. As she was walking down the path to her home, she met a bear.

"Where are you going?" asked the bear.

"I am looking for a boy to watch my cows and my sheep," she answered.

"Will you have me?"

"Yes, if you know how to call my animals gently."

"Ugh, ugh," called the bear. He tried to call softly, but he had always growled before, and now he could do nothing but growl.

"No, no," said the old woman, "your voice is too loud. Every cow in the field would run, and every sheep would hide, if you should growl like that. I will not have you."

Then the old woman went on till she met a wolf.

"Where are you going, grandmother?" he asked.

"I am looking for a boy to watch my cows and my sheep," she answered.

"Will you have me?" asked the wolf.

"Yes," she said, "if you know how to call my animals gently."

"Ho-y, ho-y," called the wolf.

"Your voice is too high," said the old woman. "My cows and my sheep would tremble whenever they heard it. I will not have you."

Then the old woman went on till she met a fox.

"I am so glad to meet you," said the fox. "Where are you going this bright morning?"

"I am going home now," she said, "for I cannot find a boy to watch my cows and my sheep. The bear growls and the wolf calls in too high a voice. I do not know what I can do, for I am too old to watch cows and sheep."

"Oh, no," said the cunning fox, "you are not old, but any one as beautiful as you must not watch sheep in the fields. I shall be very glad to do the work for you if you will let me."

"I know that my sheep will like you," said she.

"And I know that I shall like them dearly," said the fox.

"Can you call them gently, Mr. Fox?" she asked.

"Del-dal-halow, del-dal-halow," called the fox, in so gentle a voice that it was like a whisper.

"That is good, Mr. Fox," said the old woman. "Come home with me, and I will take you to the fields where my animals go."

Each day one of the cows or one of the sheep was gone when the fox came home at night. "Mr. Fox, where is my cow?" the old woman would ask, or, "Mr. Fox, where is my sheep?" and the fox would answer with a sorrowful look, "The bear came out of the woods, and he has eaten it," or, "The wolf came running through the fields, and he has eaten it."

The old woman was sorry to lose her sheep and her cows, but she thought, "Mr. Fox must be even more sorry than I. I will go out to the field and carry him a drink of cream."

She went to the field, and there stood the fox with the body of a sheep, for it was he who had killed and eaten every one that was gone. When he saw the old woman coming, he started to run away.

"You cruel, cunning fox!" she cried.

She had nothing to throw at him but the cream, so she threw that. It struck the tip of his tail, and from that day to this, the tip of the fox's tail has been as white as cream.

THE STORY OF THE FIRST FROG.

Once upon a time there was a man who had two children, a boy and a girl, whom he treated cruelly. The boy and the girl talked together one day, and the boy, Wah-wah-hoo, said to his sister, "Dear little sister, are you happy with our father?"

"No," answered the girl, whose name was Hah-hah. "He scolds me and beats me, and I can never please him."

"He was angry with me this morning," said the boy, "and he beat me till the blood came. See there!"

"Let us run away," said Hah-hah. "The beasts and the birds will be good to us. They really love us, and we can be very happy together."

That night the two children ran away from their cruel father. They went far into the forest, and at last they found a wigwam in which no one lived.

When the father found that Wah-wah-hoo and his sister were gone, he was very unhappy. He went out into the forest to see if he could find them. "If they would only come again," he said aloud, "I would do everything I could to please them."

"Do you think he tells the truth?" asked the wolf.

"I do not know," answered the mosquito. "He never treated them well when they were with him."

"Wolf," called the father, "will you tell me where my children are?"

Wah-wah-hoo had once told the wolf when a man was coming to shoot him, and so the wolf would not tell where they were.

"Mosquito," said the father, "where are my children?"

Hah-hah had once helped the mosquito to go home when the wind was too strong for him, and so the mosquito would not tell.

For a long time Wah-wah-hoo and his sister were really happy in the forest, for there was no one to scold them and to beat them, but at last there was a cold, cold winter. All the earth was covered with snow. The animals had gone, and Wah-wah-hoo could find no food. Death came and bore away the gentle Hah-hah. Wah-wah-hoo sat alone in the gloomy wigwam wailing for his sister. Then in his sadness he threw himself down from a high mountain and was killed.

All this time the father had been looking for his children, and at last he saw his son lying at the foot of the mountain. Then he too wailed and cried aloud, for he was really sorry that he had treated them so cruelly. He was a magician, and he could make his son live, but he could not make him a boy again.

"You shall be a frog," said he, "and you shall make your home in the marsh with the reeds and the rushes. There you shall wail as loud as you will for your sister, and once every moon I will come and wail for her with you. I was cruel to you and to her, and so I must live alone in my gloomy wigwam."

Every summer night one can hear the frog in the marsh wailing for his dear sister Hah-hah. Sometimes a louder voice is heard, and that is the voice of the father wailing because he was so cruel.

WHY THE RABBIT IS TIMID.

One night the moon looked down from the sky upon the people on the earth and said to herself, "How sorrowful they look! I wish I knew what troubles them. The stars and I are never sad, and I do not see why men should be troubled." She listened closely, and she heard the people say, "How happy we should be if death never came to us. Death is always before us."

The path of the moon lies across the sky, and she could not leave it to go to the earth, but she called the white rabbit and said, "Rabbit, should you be afraid to go down to the earth?"

"No," answered the rabbit, "I am not afraid."

"The people on the earth are troubled because death is before them. Now will you go to them and whisper, 'The moon dies every night. You can see it go down into the darkness, but when another night comes, then the moon rises again,'--can you remember to tell them that?"

"Yes," said the rabbit, "I will remember."

"Say this," said the moon: "'The moon dies, but the moon rises again, and so will you.'"

The rabbit was so glad to go to the earth that he danced and leaped and sprang and frolicked, but when he tried to tell the people what the moon had said, he could not remember, and he said, "The moon says that she dies and will not rise again, and so you will die and will not rise again."

The moon saw that the people were still troubled, and she called the rabbit and asked what he had said to them.

"I said that as you die and do not rise, so they too will die and not rise," said the rabbit.

"You did not try to remember, and you must be punished," said the moon, and she fired an arrow tipped with flint at the rabbit.

The arrow struck the rabbit's lip and split it. From that time every rabbit has had a split lip. The rabbit was afraid of the moon, and he was afraid of the people on the earth. He had been brave before, but now he is the most timid of animals, for he is afraid of everything and everybody.

WHY THE PEETWEET CRIES FOR RAIN.

"Come to me, every bird that flies," said the Great Father. "There is work to be done that only my birds can do."

The birds were happy that they could do something to please the Great Father, for they remembered how good he had always been to them. They flew to him eagerly to ask what they should do for him. "O Great Father," they sang all together, "tell us what we can do for you."

"The waters that I have made know not where to go," said the Father. "Some should go to the seas, some should go to the lakes in the hollows among the mountains, and some should make rivers that will dance over the rocks and through the fields on their way to the sea."

"And can even as small a bird as I show them where to go?" asked the sparrow eagerly.

"Yes," said the Father, "even my little humming-bird can help me."

Every bird that flies had come to the Father, but the peetweet had come last because he was lazy.

"I do not really wish to fly all over the earth," said he, "to show the waters where to go."

"Oh, I wish I were a bird," said a butterfly. "I should be so glad to do something for the Father."

But the peetweet went on, "I should think the lakes could find their way into the hollows of the mountains by themselves."

The Father heard the lazy peetweet, and he said, "Do you not wish to show the waters where to go?"

"They never showed me where to go," said the lazy bird. "I am not thirsty. Let whoever is thirsty and needs the water help the lakes and rivers."

The other birds all stood still in wonder. "He will be punished," they whispered.

"Yes, he must be punished," said the Father sadly. Then said he to the lazy peetweet, "Never again shall you drink of the water that is in river or lake. When you are thirsty, you must look for a hollow in the rock where the rain has fallen, and there only shall you drink."

That is why the peetweet flies over river and lake, but ever cries eagerly, "Peet-weet, peet-weet!" for that is his word for "Rain, rain!"

WHY THE BEAR HAS A SHORT TAIL.

One cold morning when the fox was coming up the road with some fish, he met the bear.

"Good-morning, Mr. Fox," said the bear.

"Good-morning, Mr. Bear," said the fox. "The morning is brighter because I have met you."

"Those are very good fish, Mr. Fox," said the bear. "I have not eaten such fish for many a day. Where do you find them?"

"I have been fishing, Mr. Bear," answered the fox.

"If I could catch such fish as those, I should like to go fishing, but I do not know how to fish."

"It would be very easy for you to learn, Mr. Bear," said the fox. "You are so big and strong that you can do anything."

"Will you teach me, Mr. Fox?" asked the bear.

"I would not tell everybody, but you are such a good friend that I will teach you. Come to this pond, and I will show you how to fish through the ice."

So the fox and the bear went to the frozen pond, and the fox showed the bear how to make a hole in the ice.

"That is easy for you," said the fox, "but many an animal could not have made that hole. Now comes the secret. You must put your tail down into the water and keep it there. That is not easy, and not every animal could do it, for the water is very cold; but you are a learned animal, Mr. Bear, and you know that the secret of catching fish is to keep your tail in the water a long time. Then when you pull it up, you will pull with it as many fish as I have."

The bear put his tail down into the water, and the fox went away. The sun rose high in the heavens, and still the bear sat with his tail through the hole in the ice. Sunset came, but still the bear sat with his tail through the hole in the ice, for he thought, "When an animal is really learned, he will not fear a little cold."

It began to be dark, and the bear said, "Now I will pull the fish out of the water. How good they will be!" He pulled and pulled, but not a fish came out. Worse than that, not all of his tail came out, for the end of it was frozen fast to the ice.

He went slowly down the road, growling angrily, "I wish I could find that fox;" but the cunning fox was curled up in his warm nest, and whenever he thought of the bear he laughed.

WHY THE WREN FLIES CLOSE TO THE EARTH.

One day when the birds were all together, one of them said, "I have been watching men, and I saw that they had a king. Let us too have a king."

"Why?" asked the others.

"Oh, I do not know, but men have one."

"Which bird shall it be? How shall we choose a king?"

"Let us choose the bird that flies farthest," said one.

"No, the bird that flies most swiftly."

"The most beautiful bird."

"The bird that sings best."

"The strongest bird."

The owl sat a little way off on a great oak-tree. He said nothing, but he looked so wise that all the birds cried, "Let us ask the owl to choose for us."

"The bird that flies highest should be our king," said the owl with a wiser look than before, and the others said, "Yes, we will choose the bird that flies highest."

The wren is very small, but she cried even more eagerly than the others, "Let us choose the bird that flies highest," for she said to herself, "They think the owl is wise, but I am wiser than he, and I know which bird can fly highest."

Then the birds tried their wings. They flew high, high up above the earth, but one by one they had to come back to their homes. It was soon seen which could fly highest, for when all the others had come back, there was the eagle rising higher and higher.

"The eagle is our king," cried the birds on the earth, and the eagle gave a loud cry of happiness. But look! A little bird had been hidden in the feathers on the eagle's back, and when the eagle had gone as high as he could, the wren flew up from his back still higher.

"Now which bird is king?" cried the wren. "The one that flew highest should be king, and I flew highest."

The eagle was angry, but not a word did he say, and the two birds came down to the earth together.

"I am the king," said the wren, "for I flew higher than the eagle." The other birds did not know which of the two to choose. At last they went to the oak-tree and asked the owl. He looked to the east, the west, the south, and the north, and then he said, "The wren did not fly at all, for she was carried on the eagle's back. The eagle is king, for he not only flew highest, but carried the wren on his back."

"Good, good!" cried the other birds. "The owl is the wisest bird that flies. We will do as he says, and the eagle shall be our king." The wren crept away. She thought she was wise before, but now she is really wise, for she always flies close to the earth, and never tries to do what she cannot.

WHY THE HOOFS OF THE DEER ARE SPLIT.

The manito of the Indians taught them how to do many things. He told them how to build wigwams, and how to hunt and to fish. He showed them how to make jars in which to keep food and water. When little children came to be with them, it was the manito who said, "See, this is the way to make soft, warm cradles for the babies."

The good spirit often comes down from his happy home in the sky to watch the Indians at their work. When each man does as well as he can, the manito is pleased, but if an Indian is lazy or wicked, the spirit is angry, and the Indian is always punished in one way or another.

One day when the manito was walking in the forest, he said to himself, "Everything is good and happy. The green leaves are whispering merrily together, the waves are lapping on the shore and laughing, the squirrels are chattering and laying up their food for winter. Everything loves me, and the colors of the flowers are brighter when I lay my hand upon them."

Then the manito heard a strange sound. "I have not often heard that," said he. "I do not like it. Some one in the forest has wicked thoughts in his heart."

Beside a great rock he saw a man with a knife.

"What are you doing with the knife?" asked the manito.

"I am throwing it away," answered the man.

"Tell me the truth," said the manito.

"I am sharpening it," replied the man.

"That is strange," said the manito, "You have food in your wigwam. Why should you sharpen a knife?"

The man could not help telling the truth to the manito, and so he answered, but greatly against his will, "I am sharpening the knife to kill the wicked animals."

"Which animal is wicked?" asked the manito. "Which one does you harm?"

"Not one does me harm," said the man, "but I do not like them. I will make them afraid of me, and I will kill them."

"You are a cruel, wicked man," said the manito. "The animals have done you no harm, and you do not need them for food. You shall no longer be a man. You shall be a deer, and be afraid of every man in the forest."

The knife fell from the man's hand and struck his foot. He leaped and stamped, but the knife only went in deeper. He cried aloud, but his voice sounded strange. His hands were no longer hands, but feet. Antlers grew from his head, and his whole body was not that of a man, but that of a deer. He runs in the forest as he will, but whenever he sees a man, he is afraid. His hoofs are split because the knife that he had made so sharp fell upon his foot when he was a man; and whenever he looks at them, he has to remember that it was his own wickedness which made him a deer.

THE STORY OF THE FIRST GRASSHOPPER.

In a country that is far away there once lived a young man called Tithonus.

He was strong and beautiful. Light of heart and light of foot, he hunted the deer or danced and sang the livelong day. Every one who saw him loved him, but the one that loved him most was a goddess named Aurora.

Every goddess had her own work, but the work of Aurora was most beautiful of all, for she was the goddess of the morning. It was she who went out to meet the sun and to light up his pathway. She watched over the flowers, and whenever they saw her coming, their colors grew brighter. She loved everything beautiful, and that is why she loved Tithonus.

"Many a year have I roamed through this country," she said to herself, "but never have I seen such bright blue eyes as those. O fairest of youths," she cried, "who are you? Some name should be yours that sounds like the wind in the pine trees, or like the song of a bird among the first blossoms."

The young man fell upon his knees before her. "I know well," said he, "that you are no maiden of the earth. You are a goddess come down to us from the skies. I am but a hunter, and I roam through the forest looking for deer."

"Come with me, fairest of hunters," said Aurora. "Come with me to the home of my father. You shall live among my brothers and hunt with them, or go with me at the first brightness of the morning to carry light and gladness to the flowers."

So it was that Tithonus went away from his own country and his own home to live in the home of Aurora.

For a long time they were happy together, but one day Aurora said, "Tithonus, I am a goddess, and so I am immortal, but some day death will bear you away from me. I will ask the father of the gods that you too may be immortal."

Then Aurora went to the king of the gods and begged that he would make Tithonus immortal.

"Sometimes people are not pleased even when I have given them what they ask," replied the king, "so think well before you speak."

"I have only one wish," said Aurora, "and it is that Tithonus, the fairest of youths, shall be immortal."

"You have your wish," said the king of the gods, and again Tithonus and Aurora roamed happily together through forest and field.

One day Tithonus asked, "My Aurora, why is it that I cannot look straight into your eyes as once I did?" Another day he said, "My Aurora, why is it that I cannot put my hand in yours as once I did?"

Then the goddess wept sorrowfully. "The king of the gods gave me what I asked for," she wailed, "and I begged that you should be immortal. I did not remember to ask that you should be always young."

Everyday Tithonus grew older and smaller. "I am no longer happy in your father's home," he said, "with your brothers who are as beautiful and as strong as I was when I first saw you. Let me go back to my own country. Let me be a bird or an insect and live in the fields where we first roamed together. Let me go, dearest goddess."

"You shall do as you will," replied Aurora sadly. "You shall be a grasshopper, and whenever I hear the grasshopper's clear, merry song, I shall remember the happy days when we were together."

THE STORY OF THE ORIOLE.

The king of the north once said to himself, "I am master of the country of ice and snow, but what is that if I cannot be ruler of the land of sunshine and flowers? I am no king if I fear the king of the south. The northwind shall bear my icy breath. Bird and beast shall quiver and tremble with cold. I myself will call in the voice of the thunder, and this ruler of the south, his king of summer, shall yield to my power."

The land of the south was ever bright and sunny, but all at once the sky grew dark, and the sun hid himself in fear. Black storm-clouds came from the north. An icy wind blew over the mountains. It wrestled with the trees of the southland, and even the oaks could not stand against its power. Their roots were tough and strong, but they had to yield, and the fallen trees lay on the earth and wailed in sorrow as the cruel storm-wind and rain beat upon them. The thunder growled in the hollows of the mountains, and in the fearful gloom came the white fire of the forked lightning, flaring through the clouds.

"We shall perish," cried the animals of the sunny south. "The arrows of the lightning are aimed at us. O dear ruler of the southland, must we yield to the cruel master of the north?"

"My king," said a little buzzing voice, "may I go out and fight the wicked master of the storm-wind?"

The thunder was still for a moment, and a mocking laugh was heard from among the clouds, for it was a little hornet that had asked to go out and meet the power of the ruler of the north.

"Dear king, may I go?" repeated the hornet.

"Yes, you may go," said the king of the south, and the little insect went out alone, and bravely stung the master of the storm-wind.

The king of the north struck at him with a war-club, but the hornet only flew above his head and stung him again. The hornet was too small to be struck by the arrows of the lightning. He stung again and again, and at last the king of the north went back to his own country, and drove before him the thunder and lightning and rain and the black storm-clouds and the icy wind.

"Brave little hornet," said the king of the south, "tell me what I can do for you.

You shall have whatever you ask."

Then said the little hornet, "My king, on all the earth no one loves me. I do not wish to harm people, but they fear my sting, and they will not let me live beside their homes. Will you make men love me?"

"Little hornet," said the king gently, "you shall no longer be a stinging insect feared by men. You shall be a bright and happy oriole, and when men see you, they will say, 'See the beautiful oriole. I shall be glad if he will build his nest on our trees.'"

So the hornet is now an oriole, a bird that is loved by every one. His nest looks like that of a hornet because he learned how to build his home before he became an oriole.

WHY THE PEACOCK'S TAIL HAS A HUNDRED EYES.

Juno, queen of the gods, had the fairest cow that any one ever saw. She was creamy white, and her eyes were of as soft and bright a blue as those of any maiden in the world. Juno and the king of the gods often played tricks on each other, and Juno knew well that the king would try to get her cow. There was a watchman named Argus, and one would think that he could see all that was going on in the world, for he had a hundred eyes, and no one had ever seen them all asleep at once, so Queen Juno gave to Argus the work of watching the white cow.

The king of the gods knew what she had done, and he laughed to himself and said, "I will play a trick on Juno, and I will have the white cow." He sent for Mercury and whispered in his ear, "Mercury, go to the green field where Argus watches the cream-white cow and get her for me."

Mercury was always happy when he could play a trick on any one, and he set out gladly for the field where Argus watched the cream-white cow with every one of his hundred eyes.

Now Mercury could tell merry stories of all that was done in the world. He could sing, too, and the music of his voice had lulled many a god to sleep. Argus knew that, but he had been alone a long time, and he thought, "What harm is there in listening to his merry chatter? I have a hundred eyes, and even if half of them were asleep, the others could easily keep watch of one cow." So he gladly hailed Mercury and said, "I have been alone in this field a long, long time, but you have roamed about as you would. Will you not sing to me, and tell me what has happened in the world? You would be glad to hear stories and music if you had nothing to do but watch a cow, even if it was the cow of a queen."

So Mercury sang and told stories. Some of the songs were merry, and some were sad. The watchman closed one eye, then another and another, but there were two eyes that would not close for all the sad songs and all the merry ones. Then Mercury drew forth a hollow reed that he had brought from the river and began to play on it. It was a magic reed, and as he played, one could hear the water rippling gently on the shore and the breath of the wind in the pine-trees; one could see the lilies bending their heads as the dusk came on, and the stars twinkling softly in the summer sky.

It is no wonder that Argus closed one eye and then the other. Every one of his hundred eyes was fast asleep, and Mercury went away to the king of the gods with the cream-white cow.

Juno had so often played tricks on the king that he was happy because he had played this one on her, but Juno was angry, and she said to Argus, "You are a strange watchman. You have a hundred eyes, and you could not keep even one of them from falling asleep. My peacock is wiser than you, for he knows when any one is looking at him. I will put every one of your eyes in the tail of the peacock." And to-day, whoever looks at the peacock can count in his tail the hundred eyes that once belonged to Argus.

THE STORY OF THE BEES AND THE FLIES.

There were once two tribes of little people who lived near together. They were not at all alike, for one of the tribes looked for food and carried it away to put it up safely for winter, while the other played and sang and danced all day long.

"Come and play with us," said the lazy people, but the busy workers answered, "No, come and work with us. Winter will soon be here. Snow and ice will be everywhere, and if we do not put up food now we shall have none for the cold, stormy days."

So the busy people brought honey from the flowers, but the lazy people kept on playing. They laughed together and whispered to one another, "See those busy workers! They will have food for two tribes, and they will give us some. Let us go and dance."

While the summer lasted, one tribe worked and the other played. When winter came, the busy workers were sorry for their friends and said, "Let us give them some of our honey." So the people who played had as much food as if they, too, had brought honey from the flowers.

Another summer was coming, and the workers said, "If we should make our home near the lilies that give us honey, it would be easier to get our food." So the workers flew away, but the lazy people played and danced as they had done before while their friends were near, for they thought, "Oh, they will come back and bring us some honey."

By and by the cold came, but the lazy people had nothing to eat, and the workers did not come with food. The manito had said to them, "Dear little workers, you shall no longer walk from flower to flower. I will give you wings, and you shall be bees. Whenever men hear a gentle humming, they will say, 'Those are the busy bees, and their wings were given them because they were wise and good.'"

To the other tribe the manito said, "You shall be flies, and you, too, shall have wings; but while the workers fly from flower to flower and eat the yellow honey, you shall have for your food only what has been thrown away. When men hear your buzzing, they will say, 'It is good that the flies have wings, because we can drive them away from us the more quickly.'"

THE STORY OF THE FIRST MOLES.

A rich man and a poor man once owned a field together. The rich man owned the northern half, and the poor man owned the southern half. Each man sowed his ground with seed. The warm days came, the gentle rain fell, and the seed in the poor man's half of the field sprang up and put forth leaves. The seed in the rich man's half all died in the ground.

The rich man was selfish and wicked. He said, "The southern half of the field is mine," but the poor man replied, "No, the southern half is mine, for that is where I sowed my seed."

The rich man had a son who was as wicked as himself. This boy whispered, "Father, tell him to come in the morning. I know how we can keep the land." So the rich man said, "Come in the morning, and we shall soon see whose land this is."

At night the rich man and his son pulled up some bushes that grew beside the field, and the son hid in the hole where their roots had been.

Morning came, and many people went to the field with the rich man. The poor man was sorrowful, for he feared that he would lose his ground.

"Now we shall see," said the rich man boastfully, and he called aloud, "Whose ground is this?"

"This is the ground of the rich man," answered a voice from the hole.

"How shall I ever get food for my children!" cried the poor man.

Then another voice was heard. It was that of the spirit of the fields, and it said, "The southern half of the field is the poor man's, and the northern half shall be his too."

The rich man would have run away, but the voice called, "Wait. Look where the bushes once stood. The boy in the hole and his wicked father shall hide in the darkness as long as they live, and never again shall they see the light of the sun."

This is the story of the first moles, and this is why the mole never comes to the light of day.

THE STORY OF THE FIRST ANTS.

"This jar is full of smoked flesh," said one voice.

"This has fish, this is full of honey, and that one is almost running over with oil," said another voice. "We shall have all that we need to eat for many days to come."

These are the words that a villager coming home from his work heard his mother and his sister say.

"They have often played tricks on me," he said to himself, "and now I will play one on them." So he went into the house and said, "Mother, I have found that I have a wonderful sense of smell, and by its help I can find whatever is hidden away."

"That is a marvelous story," cried the sister.

"If you can tell me what is in these jars," said his mother, "I shall think you are really a magician. What is it now?"

"This is flesh, this fish, this honey, and this jar is full of oil," said the man.

"I never heard of such a marvel in all my life," cried the mother; and in the morning she called her friends and said, "Only think what a wonderful sense of smell my son has! He told me what was in these jars when they were closed."

It was not long before the people all through the country heard of the wonderful man, and one day word came that the king wished to see him at once.

The man was afraid, for he did not know what would happen to him, and he was still more afraid when the king said, "A pearl is lost that I had in my hand last night. They say you can find things that are lost. Find my pearl, or your head will he lost."

The poor man went out into the forest. "Oh, how I wish I had not tried to play tricks," he wailed. "Then this sharp sorrow, this dire trouble, would not have come upon me."

"Please, please do not tell the king," said two voices in the shadow of the trees.

"Who are you?" asked the man.

"Oh, you must know us well," said a man coming out into the light. "My name is Sharp, and that man behind the tree is named Dire, but please do not tell the king. We will give you the pearl; here it is. You called our names, and we saw that you knew us. Oh, I wish I had not been a thief!"

The man gave the pearl to the king, and went home wishing that no one would ever talk to him again of his sense of smell.

In three days word came from the queen that he must come to her at once.

She thought his power was only a trick, and to catch him she had put a cat into a bag and the bag into a box.

When the man came, she asked sharply, "What is in this box? Tell me the truth, or off will go your head."

"What shall I do?" thought the man, "Dire death is upon me." He did not remember that he was before the queen, and he repeated half aloud an old saying, "The bagged cat soon dies."

"What is that?" cried the queen.

"The bagged cat soon dies," repeated the man in great terror.

"You are a marvelous man," said the queen. "There is really a bag in the box and a cat in the bag, but no one besides myself knew it."

"He is not a man; he is a god," cried the people, "and he must be in the sky and live among the gods;" so they threw him up to the sky. His hand was full of earth, and when the earth fell back, it was no longer earth, but a handful of ants. Ants have a wonderful sense of smell, and it is because they fell from the hand of this man who was thrown up into the sky to live among the gods.

THE FACE OF THE MANITO.

Many years ago the manito of the Indians lived in the sun. Every morning the wise men of the tribe went to the top of a mountain, and as the sun rose in the east, they sang, "We praise thee, O sun! From thee come fire and light. Be good to us, be good to us."

After the warm days of the summer had come, the sun was so bright that the Indians said to their wise men, "When you go to the mountain top, ask the manito to show us his face in a softer, gentler light."

Then the wise men went to the mountain top, and this is what they said: "O great manito, we are but children before you, and we have no power to bear the brightness of your face. Look down upon us here on the earth with a gentler, softer light, that we may ever gaze upon you and show you all love and all honor."

The bright sun moved slowly toward the south. The people were afraid that the manito was angry with them, but when the moon rose they were no longer sad, for from the moon the loving face of the manito was looking down upon them.

Night after night the people gazed at the gentle face, but at last a night came when the moon was not seen in the sky. The wise men went sorrowfully to the mountain top. "O manito," they said, "we are never happy when we cannot gaze into your face. Will you not show it to your children?"

The moon did not rise, and the people were sad, but when morning came, there was the loving face of the manito showing clearly in the rocks at the top of the mountain.

Again they were happy, but when dark clouds hid the gentle face, the wise men went to the foot of the mountain and called sadly, "O manito, we can no longer see your face."

The clouds grew darker and fell like a cloak over the mountain, the trees trembled in the wind, the forked lightning shot across the sky, and the thunder called aloud.

"It is the anger of the manito," cried the people. "The heavens are falling," they whispered, and they hid their faces in fear.

Morning came, the storm had gone, and the sky was clear. Tremblingly the people looked up toward the mountain top for the face of the manito. It was not there, but after they had long gazed in sorrow, a wise man cried, "There it is, where no cloud will hide it from us." In the storm the rocks had fallen from the mountain top. They were halfway down the mountain side, and in them could be seen the face of the manito.

Then the people cried, "Praise to the good manito! His loving face will look down upon us from the mountain side forever-more."

For a long time all went well, but at last trouble came, for they heard that a great tribe were on the war-path coming to kill them. "Help us, dear manito," they cried but there was no help. The warriors came nearer and nearer. Their war-cry was heard, "O manito," called the people, "help us, help us!" A voice from the mountain answered, "My children, be not afraid." The war-cry was still, and when the people looked, for the warriors, they were nowhere to be seen. The people gazed all around, and at last one of the wise men cried, "There they are, there they are!"

They were at the foot of the mountain, but the people no longer feared them, for now they were not warriors but rocks. To keep from harm those whom he loved, the manito had made the warriors into stone. They stood at the foot of the mountain, and to-day, if you should go to that far-away country, you could see the rocks that were once warriors, and above them, halfway up the mountain side, you could see the face of the manito.

THE STORY OF THE FIRST DIAMONDS.

The chief of an Indian tribe had two sons whom he loved very dearly. This chief was at war with another tribe, and one dark night two of his enemies crept softly through the trees till they came to where the two boys lay sound asleep. The warriors caught the younger boy up gently, and carried him far away from his home and his friends.

When the chief woke, he cried, "Where is my son? My enemies have been here and have stolen him."

All the Indians in the tribe started out in search of the boy. They roamed the forest through and through, but the stolen child could not be found.

The chief mourned for his son, and when the time of his death drew near, he said to his wife, "Moneta, my tribe shall have no chief until my boy is found and taken from our enemies. Let our oldest son go forth in search of his brother, and until he has brought back the little one, do you rule my people."

Moneta ruled the people wisely and kindly. When the older son was a man she said to him, "My son, go forth and search for your brother, whom I have mourned these many years. Every day I shall watch for you, and every night I shall build a fire on the mountain top."

"Do not mourn, mother," said the young man. "You will not build the fire many nights on the mountain top, for I shall soon find my brother and bring him back to you."

He went forth bravely, but he did not come back. His mother went every night to the mountain top, and when she was so old that she could no longer walk, the young men of the tribe bore her up the mountain side in their strong arms, so that with her own trembling hand she could light the fire.

One night there was a great storm. Even the brave warriors were afraid, but Moneta had no fear, for out of the storm a gentle voice had come to her that said, "Moneta, your sons are coming home to you."

"Once more I must build the fire on the mountain top," she cried. The young men trembled with fear, but they bore her to the top of the mountain.

"Leave me here alone," she said. "I hear a voice. It is the voice of my son, and he is calling, 'Mother, mother.' Come to me, come, my boys."

Coming slowly up the mountain in the storm was the older son. The younger had died on the road home, and he lay dead in the arms of his brother.

In the morning the men of the tribe went to the mountain top in search of Moneta and her sons. They were nowhere to be seen, but where the tears of the lonely mother had fallen, there was a brightness that had never been seen before. The tears were shining in the sunlight as if each one of them was itself a little sun. Indeed, they were no longer tears, but diamonds.

The dearest thing in all the world is the tear of mother-love, and that is why the tears were made into diamonds, the stones that are brightest and clearest of all the stones on the earth.

THE STORY OF THE FIRST PEARLS.

There was once a man named Runoia, and when he walked along the pathways of the forest, the children would say shyly to one another, "Look, there is the man who always hears music."

It was really true that wherever he went he could hear sweet music. There are some kinds of music that every one can hear, but Runoia heard sweet sounds where others heard nothing. When the lilies sang their evening song to the stars, he could hear it, and when the mother tree whispered "Good-night" to the little green leaves, he heard the music of her whisper, though other men heard not a sound.

He was sorry for those other men, and he said to himself, "I will make a harp, and then even if they cannot hear all the kinds of music, they will hear the sweet voice of the harp."

This must have been a magic harp, for if one else touched it, no sound was heard, but when Runoia touched the strings, the trees bent down their branches to listen, the little blossoms put their heads out shyly, and even the wind was hushed. All kinds of beasts and birds came about him as he played, and the sun and the moon stood still in the heavens to hear the wonderful music. All these beautiful things happened whenever Runoia touched the strings.

Sometimes Runoia's music was sad. Then the sun and the moon hid their faces behind the clouds, the wind sang mournfully, and the lilies bent low their snow-white blossoms.

One day Runoia roamed far away till he came to the shores of the great sea. The sun had set, darkness hid the sky and the water, not a star was to be seen. Not a sound was heard but the wailing of the sea. No friend was near. "I have no friends," he said. He laid his hand upon his harp, and of themselves the strings gave forth sweet sounds, at first softly and shyly. Then the sounds grew louder, and soon the world was full of music, such as even Runoia had never heard before, for it was the music of the gods. "It is really true," he said to himself softly. "My harp is giving me music to drive away my sadness."

He listened, and the harp played more and more sweetly. "He who has a harp has one true friend. He who loves music is loved by the gods," so the harp sang to him.

Tears came into Runoia's eyes, but they were tears of happiness, not of sadness, for he was no longer lonely. A gentle voice called, "Runoia, come to the home of the gods."

As darkness fell over the sea, Runoia's friends went to look for him. He was gone, but where he had stood listening happily to the music of the gods, there on the fair white sand was the harp, and all around it lay beautiful pearls, shining softly in the moonlight, for every tear of happiness was now a pearl.

THE STORY OF THE FIRST EMERALDS.

In the days of long ago there was a time when there were no emeralds on the earth. Men knew where to find other precious stones. They could get pearls and diamonds, but no one had ever seen an emerald, because the emeralds were hidden away in the bed of the sea, far down below the waves.

The king of India had many precious things, and he was always eager to get others. One day a stranger stood before his door, and when the king came out he cried, "O king, you have much that is precious. Do you wish to have the most beautiful thing in earth, air, or water?"

"Yes, in truth," said the king. "What is it?"

"It is a vase made of an emerald stone," answered the stranger.

"And what is an emerald stone?" asked the king.

"It is a stone that no one on earth has ever seen," said the stranger. "It is greener than the waves of the sea or the leaves of the forest."

"Where is the wonderful vase?" cried the king eagerly.

"Where the waves of the sea never roll," was the answer, but when the king was about to ask where that was, the stranger had gone.

The king asked his three wise men where it was that the waves of the sea never rolled. One said, "In the forest;" another said, "On the mountain;" and the last said, "In the sea where the water is deepest."

The king thought a long time about these answers of the wise men. At last he said: "If the emerald vase had been in the forest or on the mountain, it would have been found long before now. I think it is in the deepest water of the sea."

This king of India was a great magician. He went to the sea, and there he sang many a magical song, for he said to himself, "I have no diver who can go to the bed of the sea, but often magic will do what a diver cannot."

The king of the world under the water owned the beautiful vase, but when he heard the songs, he knew that he must give it up. "Take it," he said to the spirits that live in the deepest water. "Bear it to the king of India. The spirits of the air will try to take it from you, but see that it goes safely to the king whose magic has called it from the sea."

The spirits of the sea rose from the waves bearing the precious vase.

"It is ours, it is ours," cried the spirits of the air. "The king of India shall never have it." The spirits of the air and the spirits of the water fought together. "What a fearful storm!" cried the people on the earth. "See how the lightning shoots across the sky, and hear the thunder roll from mountain to mountain!" They hid themselves in terror, but it was no storm, it was only the spirits fighting for the emerald vase.

One of the spirits of the air bore it at last far up above the top of the highest mountain. "It is mine," he cried. "Never," said a spirit of the water, and he caught it and threw it angrily against the rocky top of the mountain. It fell in hundreds of pieces.

There was no vase like it in the east or the west, the north or the south, and so the king of India never had an emerald vase; but from the pieces of the vase that was thrown against the mountain came all the emeralds that are now on the earth.

WHY THE EVERGREEN TREES NEVER LOSE THEIR LEAVES.

Winter was coming, and the birds had flown far to the south, where the air was warm and they could find berries to eat. One little bird had broken its wing and could not fly with the others. It was alone in the cold world of frost and snow. The forest looked warm, and it made its way to the trees as well as it could, to ask for help.

First it came to a birch-tree. "Beautiful birch-tree," it said, "my wing is broken, and my friends have flown away. May I live among your branches till they come back to me?"

"No, indeed," answered the birch-tree, drawing her fair green leaves away. "We of the great forest have our own birds to help. I can do nothing for you."

"The birch is not very strong," said the little bird to itself, "and it might be that she could not hold me easily. I will ask the oak." So the bird said, "Great oak-tree, you are so strong, will you not let me live on your boughs till my friends come back in the springtime?"

"In the springtime!" cried the oak. "That is a long way off. How do I know what you might do in all that time? Birds are always looking for something to eat, and you might even eat up some of my acorns."

"It may be that the willow will be kind to me," thought the bird, and it said, "Gentle willow, my wing is broken, and I could not fly to the south with the other birds. May I live on your branches till the springtime?"

The willow did not look gentle then, for she drew herself up proudly and said, "Indeed, I do not know you, and we willows never talk to people whom we do not know. Very likely there are trees somewhere that will take in strange birds. Leave me at once."

The poor little bird did not know what to do. Its wing was not yet strong, but it began to fly away as well as it could. Before it had gone far, a voice was heard. "Little bird," it said, "where are you going?"

"Indeed, I do not know," answered the bird sadly. "I am very cold."

"Come right here, then," said the friendly spruce-tree, for it was her voice that had called. "You shall live on my warmest branch all winter if you choose."

"Will you really let me?" asked the little bird eagerly.

"Indeed, I will," answered the kind-hearted spruce-tree. "If your friends have flown away, it is time for the trees to help you. Here is the branch where my leaves are thickest and softest."

"My branches are not very thick," said the friendly pine-tree, "but I am big and strong, and I can keep the north wind from you and the spruce."

"I can help too," said a little juniper-tree. "I can give you berries all winter long, and every bird knows that juniper berries are good."

So the spruce gave the lonely little bird a home, the pine kept the cold north wind away from it, and the juniper gave it berries to eat.

The other trees looked on and talked together wisely.

"I would not have strange birds on my boughs," said the birch.

"I shall not give my acorns away for any one," said the oak.

"I never have anything to do with strangers," said the willow, and the three trees drew their leaves closely about them.

In the morning all those shining green leaves lay on the ground, for a cold north wind had come in the night, and every leaf that it touched fell from the tree.

"May I touch every leaf in the forest?" asked the wind in its frolic.

"No," said the frost king. "The trees that have been kind to the little bird with the broken wing may keep their leaves."

This is why the leaves of the spruce, the pine, and the juniper are always green.

WHY THE ASPEN LEAVES TREMBLE.

"It is very strange," whispered one reed to another, "that the queen bee never guides her swarm to the aspen-tree."

"Indeed, it is strange," said the other. "The oak and the willow often have swarms, but I never saw one on the aspen. What can be the reason?"

"The queen bee cannot bear the aspen," said the first. "Very likely she has some good reason for despising it. I do not think that an insect as wise as she would despise a tree without any reason. Many wicked things happen that no one knows."

The reeds did not think that any one could hear what they said, but both the willow and the aspen heard every word. The aspen was so angry that it trembled from root to tip. "I'll soon see why that proud queen bee despises me," it said. "She shall guide a swarm to my branches or"--

"Oh, I would not care for what those reeds say," the willow-tree broke in. "They are the greatest chatterers in the world. They are always whispering together, and they always have something unkind to say."

The aspen-tree was too angry to be still, and it called out to the reeds, "You are only lazy whisperers. I do not care what you say. I despise both you and your queen bee. The honey that those bees make is not good to eat. I would not have it a anywhere near me."

"Hush, hush," whispered the willow timidly. "The reeds will repeat every word that you say."

"I do not care if they do," said the aspen. "I despise both them and the bees."

The reeds did whisper the angry words of the aspen to the queen bee, and she said, "I was going to guide my swarm to the aspen, but now I will drive the tree out of the forest. Come, my bees, come."

Then the bees flew by hundreds upon the aspen. They stung every leaf and every twig through and through. The tree was driven from the forest, over the prairie, over the river, over the fields; and still the angry bees flew after it and stung it again and again. When they had come to the rocky places, they left it and flew back to the land of flowers. The aspen never came back. Its bright green leaves had grown white through fear, and from that day to this they have trembled as they did when the bees were stinging them and driving the tree from the forest.

HOW THE BLOSSOMS CAME TO THE HEATHER.

Only a little while after the earth was made, the trees and plants came to live on it. They were happy and contented. The lily was glad because her flowers were white. The rose was glad because her flowers were red. The violet was happy because, however shyly she might hide herself away, some one would come to look for her and praise her fragrance. The daisy was happiest of all because every child in the world loved her.

The trees and plants chose homes for themselves. The oak said, "I will live in the broad fields and by the roads, and travelers may sit in my shadow." "I shall be contented on the waters of the pond," said the water-lily. "And I am contented in the sunny fields," said the daisy. "My fragrance shall rise from beside some mossy stone," said the violet. Each plant chose its home where it would be most happy and contented.

There was one little plant, however, that had not said a word and had not chosen a home. This plant was the heather. She had not the sweet fragrance of the violet, and the children did not love her as they did the daisy. The reason was that no blossoms had been given to her, and she was too shy to ask for any.

"I wish there was some one who would be glad to see me," she said; but she was a brave little plant, and she did her best to be contented and to look bright and green.

One day she heard the mountain say, "Dear plants, will you not come to my rocks and cover them with your brightness and beauty? In the winter they are cold, and in the summer they are stung by the sunshine. Will you not come and cover them?"

"I cannot leave the pond," cried the water-lily.

"I cannot leave the moss," said the violet.

"I cannot leave the green fields," said the daisy.

The little heather was really trembling with eagerness. "If the great, beautiful mountain would only let me come!" she thought, and at last she whispered very softly and shyly, "Please, dear mountain, will you let me come? I have not any blossoms like the others, but I will try to keep the wind and the sun away from you."

"Let you?" cried the mountain. "I shall be contented and happy if a dear little plant like you will only come to me."

The heather soon covered the rocky mountain side with her bright green, and the mountain called proudly to the other plants, "See how beautiful my little heather is!" The others replied, "Yes, she is bright and green, but she has no blossoms."

Then a sweet, gentle voice was heard saying, "Blossoms you shall have, little heather. You shall have many and many a flower, because you have loved the lonely mountain, and have done all that you could to please him and make him happy." Even before the sweet voice was still, the little heather was bright with many blossoms, and blossoms she has had from that day to this.

HOW FLAX WAS GIVEN TO MEN.

"You have been on the mountain a long time," said the wife of the hunter.

"Yes, wife, and I have seen the most marvelous sight in all the world," replied the hunter.

"What was that?"

"I came to a place on the mountain where I had been many and many a time before, but a great hole had been made in the rock, and through the hole I saw--oh, wife, it was indeed a wonderful sight!"

"But what was it, my hunter?"

"There was a great hall, all shining and sparkling with precious stones. There were diamonds and pearls and emeralds, more than we could put into our little house, and among all the beautiful colors sat a woman who was fairer than they. Her maidens were around her, and the hall was as bright with their beauty as it was with the stones. One was playing on a harp, one was singing, and others were dancing as lightly and merrily as a sunbeam on a blossom. The woman was even more beautiful than the maidens, and, wife, as soon as I saw her I thought that she was no mortal woman."

"Did you not fall on your knees and ask her to be good to us?"

"Yes, wife, and straightway she said: 'Rise, my friend. I have a gift for you. Choose what you will to carry to your wife as a gift from Holda.'"

"Did you choose pearls or diamonds?"

"I looked about the place, and it was all so sparkling that I closed my eyes. 'Choose your gift,' she said. I looked into her face, and then I knew that it was indeed the goddess Holda, queen of the sky. When I looked at her, I could not think of precious stones, for her eyes were more sparkling than diamonds, and I said: 'O goddess Holda, there is no gift in all your magic hall that I would so gladly bear away to my home as the little blue flower in your lily-white hand.'"

"Well!" cried the wife, "and when you might have had half the pearls and emeralds in the place, you chose a little faded blue flower! I did think you were a wiser man."

"The goddess said I had chosen well," said the hunter. "She gave me the flower and the seed of it, and she said, 'When the springtime comes, plant the seed, and in the summer I myself will come and teach you what to do with the plant.'"

In the spring the little seeds were put into the ground. Soon the green leaves came up; then many little blue flowers, as blue as the sky, lifted up their heads in the warm sunshine of summer. No one on the earth knew how to spin or to weave, but on the brightest, sunniest day of the summer, the goddess Holda came down from the mountain to the little house.

"Can you spin flax?" she asked of the wife.

"Indeed, no," said the wife.

"Can you weave linen?"

"Indeed, no."

"Then I will teach you how to spin and to weave," said the good goddess. "The little blue flower is the flax. It is my own flower, and I love the sight of it."

So the goddess sat in the home of the hunter and his wife and taught them how to spin flax and weave linen. When the wife saw the piece of linen on the grass, growing whiter and whiter the longer the sun shone upon it, she said to her husband, "Indeed, my hunter, the linen is fairer than the pearls, and I should rather have the beautiful white thing that is on the grass in the sunshine than all the diamonds in the hall of the goddess."

WHY THE JUNIPER HAS BERRIES.

Three cranberries once lived together in a meadow. They were sisters, but they did not look alike, for one was white, and one was red, and one was green. Winter came, and the wind blew cold. "I wish we lived nearer the wigwam," said the white cranberry timidly. "I am afraid that Hoots, the bear, will come. What should we do?"

"The women in the wigwam are afraid as well as we," the red cranberry said. "I heard them say they wished the men would come back from the hunt."

"We might hide in the woods," the green cranberry whispered.

"But the bear will come down the path through the woods," replied the white cranberry.

"I think our own meadow is the best place," the red cranberry said. "I shall not go away from the meadow. I shall hide here in the moss."

"I am so white," the white cranberry wailed, "that I know Hoots would see me. I shall hide in the hominy. That is as white as I."

"I cannot hide in the hominy," said the green cranberry, "but I have a good friend in the woods. I am going to ask the juniper-tree to hide me. Will you not go with me?" But the red cranberry thought it best to stay in the moss, and the white cranberry thought it best to hide in the hominy, so the green cranberry had to go alone to the friendly juniper-tree.

By and by a growling was heard, and soon Hoots himself came in sight. He walked over and over the red cranberry that lay hidden in the moss. Then he went to the wigwam. There stood the hominy, and in it was the white cranberry, trembling so she could not keep still.

"Ugh, ugh, what good hominy!" said Hoots, and in the twinkling of an eye he had eaten it up, white cranberry and all.

Now the red cranberry was dead, and the white cranberry was dead, but the little green cranberry that went to the juniper-tree had hidden away in the thick branches, and Hoots did not find her. She was so happy with the kind-hearted tree that she never left it, and that is the reason why the juniper-tree has berries.

WHY THE SEA IS SALT.

Frothi, king of the Northland, owned some magic millstones. Other millstones grind corn, but these would grind out whatever the owner wished, if he knew how to move them. Frothi tried and tried, but they would not stir.

"Oh, if I could only move the millstones," he cried, "I would grind out so many good things for my people. They should all be happy and rich."

One day King Frothi was told that two strange women were begging at the gate to see him.

"Let them come in," he said, and the were brought before him.

"We have come from a land that is far away," they said.

"What can I do for you?" asked the king.

"We have come to do something for you," answered the women.

"There is only one thing that I wish for," said the king, "and that is to make the magic millstones grind, but you cannot do that."

"Why not?" asked the women. "That is just what we have come to do. That is why we stood at your gate and begged to speak to you."

Then the king was a happy man indeed. "Bring in the millstones," he called. "Quick, quick! Do not wait." The millstones were brought in, and the women asked, "What shall we grind for you?"

"Grind gold and happiness and rest for my people," cried the king gladly.

The women touched the magic millstones, and how they did grind! "Gold and happiness and rest for the people," said the women to one another. "Those are good wishes."

The gold was so bright and yellow that King Frothi could not bear to let it go out of his sight. "Grind more," he said to the women. "Grind faster. Why did you come to my gate if you did not wish to grind?"

"We are so weary," said the women. "Will you not let us rest?"

"You may rest for as long a time as it needs to say 'Frothi,'" cried the king, "and no longer. Now you have rested. Grind away. No one should be weary who is grinding out yellow gold."

"He is a wicked king," said the women. "We will grind for him no more. Mill, grind out hundreds and hundreds of strong warriors to fight Frothi and punish him for his cruel words."

The millstones ground faster and faster. Hundreds of warriors sprang out, and they killed Frothi and all his men.

"Now I shall be king," cried the strongest of the warriors. He put the two women and the magic millstones on a ship to go to a far-away land. "Grind, grind," he called to the women.

"But we are so weary. Please let us rest," they begged.

"Rest? No. Grind on, grind on. Grind salt, if you can grind nothing else."

Night came and the weary women were still grinding. "Will you not let us rest?" they asked.

"No," cried the cruel warrior. "Keep grinding, even if the ship goes to the bottom of the sea." The women ground, and it was not long before the ship really did go to the bottom, and carried the cruel warrior with it. There at the bottom of the sea are the two millstones still grinding salt, for there is no one to say that they must grind no longer. That is why the sea is salt.

THE STORY OF THE FIRST WHITEFISH.

One day a crane was sitting on a rock far out in the water, when he heard a voice say, "Grandfather Crane, Grandfather Crane, please come and carry us across the lake." It was the voice of a child, and when the crane had come to the shore, he saw two little boys holding each other's hands and crying bitterly.

"Why do you cry?" asked the crane, "and why do you wish to go across the lake, away from your home and friends?"

"We have no friends," said the little boys, crying more bitterly than ever. "We have no father and no mother, and a cruel witch troubles us. She tries all the time to do us harm, and we are going to run away where she can never find us."

"I will carry you over the lake," said the crane. "Hold on well, but do not touch the back of my head, for if you do, you will fall into the water and go to the bottom of the lake. Will you obey me?"

"Yes, indeed, we will obey," they said. "We will not touch your head. But please come quickly and go as fast as you can. We surely heard the voice of the witch in the woods."

It really was the witch, and she was saying over and over to herself, "I will catch them, and I will punish them so that they will never run away from me again. They will obey me after I have caught them."

The crane bore the two little boys gently to the other shore, and when he came back, there stood the witch.

"Dear, gentle crane," she said, "you are so good to every one. Will you carry me over the lake? My two dear children are lost in the woods, and I have cried bitterly for them all day long."

The spirit of the lake had told the crane to carry across the lake every one that asked to be taken over; so he said, "Yes, I will carry you across. Hold on well, but do not touch the back of my head, for if you do, you will fall into the water and go to the bottom of the lake. Will you obey me?"

"Yes, indeed, I will," said the witch; but she thought, "He would not be so timid about letting me touch the back of his head if he were not afraid of my magic. I will put my hand on his head, and then he will always be in my power." So when they were far out over the lake, she put her hand on the crane's head, and before she could say "Oh!" she was at the bottom of the lake.

"You shall never live in the light again," said the crane, "for you have done no good on earth. You shall be a whitefish, and you shall be food for the Indians as long as they eat fish."

WAS IT THE FIRST TURTLE?

Once upon a time there was a great fight between two tribes of Indians. It was so fierce that the river ran red with blood, and the war-cries were so loud and angry that the animals of the forest ran away in terror. The warriors fought all day long, and when it began to grow dark, all the men on one side had been killed but two warriors, one of whom was known as Turtle. In those days there were no such animals as turtles in the ponds and rivers, and no one knew why he was called by that name. At last Turtle's friend was struck by an arrow and fell to the ground.

"Now yield!" cried the enemies.

"Friend," said Turtle, "are you dead?"

"No," said his friend.

"Then I will fight on," said Turtle, and he called out, "Give life again to the warriors whom you have killed with your wicked arrows, and then I will yield, but never before. Come on, cowards that you are! You are afraid of me. You do not dare to come!"

Then his enemies said, "We will all shoot our arrows at once, and some one of them will be sure to kill him." They made ready to fire, but Turtle, too, made ready. He had two thick shields, and he put one over his back and one over his breast. Then he called to his fierce enemies, "Are you not ready? Come on, fierce warriors! Shoot your arrows through my breast if you can."

The warriors all shot, but not an arrow struck Turtle, for the two shields covered his breast and his back, and whenever an arrow buzzed through the air, he drew in his head and his arms between the shields, and so he was not harmed. "Why do you not aim at me?" he cried. "Are you shooting at the mountain, or at the sun and the moon? Good fighters you are, indeed! Try again."

His enemies shot once more, and this time an arrow killed the wounded friend as he lay on the ground. When Turtle cried, "Friend, are you living?" there was no answer.

"My friend is dead," said Turtle. "I will fight no more."

"He has yielded," cried his enemies.

"He has not," said Turtle, and with one great leap he sprang into the river. His enemies did not dare to spring after him.

"Those long arms of his would pull us to the bottom," they said; "but we will watch till he comes up, and then we shall be sure of him."

They were not so sure as they thought, for he did not come up, and all that they could see in the water was a strange creature unlike anything that had been there before.

"It has arms and a head," said one.

"And it pulls them out of sight just as Turtle did," said another.

"It has a shield over its back and one over its breast, as Turtle had," said the first. Then all the warriors were so eager to watch the strange animal that they no longer remembered the fight. They crowded up to the shore of the river.

"It is not Turtle," cried one.

"It is Turtle," declared another.

"It is so like him that I do not care to go into the water as long as it is in sight," said still another.

"But if this is not Turtle, where is he?" they all asked, and not one of the wise men of their tribe could answer.

WHY THE CROCODILE HAS A WIDE MOUTH.

"Come to my kingdom whenever you will," said the goddess of the water to the king of the land. "My waves will be calm, and my animals will be gentle. They will be as good to your children as if they were my own. Nothing in all my kingdom will do you harm."

The goddess went back to her home in the sea, and the king walked to the shore of the river and stood gazing upon the beautiful water. Beside him walked his youngest son.

"Father," asked the boy, "would the goddess be angry if I went into the water to swim?"

"No," answered the father. "She says that nothing in all her wide kingdom will do us harm. The water-animals will be kind, and the waves will be calm."

The boy went into the water. He could swim as easily as a fish, and he went from shore to shore, sometimes talking with the fishes, sometimes getting a bright piece of stone to carry to his father. Suddenly something caught him by the foot and dragged him down, down, through the deep, dark water. "Oh, father!" he cried, but his father had gone away from the shore, and the strange creature, whatever it was, dragged the boy down to the very bottom of the river.

The river was full of sorrow for what the creature had done, and it lifted the boy gently and bore him to the feet of the goddess. His eyes were closed and his face was white, for he was dead. Great tears came from the eyes of the goddess when she looked at him. "I did not think any of my animals would do such a cruel thing," she said. "His father shall never know it, for the boy shall not remember what has happened."

Then she laid her warm hand upon his head, and whispered some words of magic into his ear. "Open your eyes," she called, and soon they were wide open. "You went in to swim," said the goddess. "Did the water please you?"

"Yes, surely."

"Were the water-animals kind to you?"

"Yes, surely," answered the boy, for the magic words had kept him from remembering anything about the strange creature that had dragged him to the bottom of the river.

The boy went home to his father, and as soon as he was out of sight, the goddess called to the water-animals, "Come one, come all, come little, come great."

"It is the voice of the goddess," said the water-animals, and they all began to swim toward her as fast as they could.

When they were together before her, she said, "One of you has been cruel and wicked. One of you has dragged to the bottom of the river the son of my friend, the king of the land, but I have carried him safely to shore, and now he is in his home. When he comes again, will you watch over him wherever in the wide, wide water he may wish to go?"

"Yes!" "Yes!" "Yes!" cried the water-animals.

"Water," asked the goddess, "will you be calm and still when the son of my friend is my guest?"

"Gladly," answered the water.

Suddenly the goddess caught sight of the crocodile hiding behind the other animals. "Will you be kind to the boy and keep harm away from him?" she asked.

Now it was the crocodile that had dragged the boy to the bottom of the river. He wished to say, "Yes," but he did not dare to open his mouth for fear of saying, "I did it, I did it," so he said not a word. The goddess cried, "Did you drag the king's son to the bottom of the river?" Still the crocodile dared not open his mouth for fear of saying, "I did it, I did it." Then the goddess was angry. She drew her long sword, and saying, "The mouth that will not open when it should must be made to open," she struck the crocodile's mouth with the sword. "Oh, look!" cried the other animals. The crocodile's mouth had opened; there was no question about that, for it had split open so far that he was afraid he should never be able to keep it closed.

THE STORY OF THE PICTURE ON THE VASE.

On some of the beautiful vases that are made in Japan there is a picture of a goddess changing a dragon into an island. When the children of Japan say, "Mother, tell us a story about the picture," this is what the mother says:--

"Long, long ago there was a goddess of the sea who loved the people of Japan. She often came out of the water at sunset, and while all the bright colors were in the sky, she would sit on a high rock that overlooked the water and tell stories to the children. Such wonderful stories as they were! She used to tell them all about the strange fishes that swim in and out among the rocks and the mosses, and about the fair maidens that live deep down in the sea far under the waves. The children would ask, 'Are there no children in the sea? Why do they never come out to play with us?' The goddess would answer, 'Some time they will come, if you only keep on wishing for them. What children really wish for they will surely have some day.'

"Then the goddess would sing to the children, and her voice was so sweet that the evening star would stand still in the sky to listen to her song. 'Please show us how the water rises and falls,' the children would beg, and she would hold up a magic stone that she had and say, 'Water, rise!' Then the waves would come in faster and faster all about the rock. When she laid down the stone and said, 'Water, fall!' the waves would be still, and the water would roll back quickly to the deep sea. She was goddess of the storm as well as of the sea, and sometimes the children would say, 'Dear goddess, please make us a storm.' She never said no to what they asked, and so the rain would fall, the lightning flare, and the thunder roll. The rain would fall all about them, but the goddess did not let it come near them. They were never afraid of the lightning, for it was far above their heads, and they knew that the goddess would not let it come down.

"Those were happy times, but there is something more to tell that is not pleasant. One of the goddess's sea-animals was a dragon, that often used to play in the water near the shore. The children never thought of being afraid of any of the sea-animals, but one day the cruel dragon seized a little child in his mouth, and in a moment he had eaten it. There was sadness over the land of Japan. There were tears and sorrowful wailing. 'O goddess,' the people cried, 'come to us! Punish the wicked dragon!'

"The goddess was angry that one of her creatures should have dared to harm the little child, and she called aloud, 'Dragon, come to me.' The dragon came in a moment, for he did not dare to stay away. Then said the goddess, 'You shall never again play merrily in the water with the happy sea-animals. You shall be a rocky island. There shall be trees and plants on you, and before many years have gone, people will no longer remember that you were once an animal.'

"The dragon found that he could no longer move about as he had done, for he was changing into rock. Trees and plants grew on his back. He was an island, and when people looked at it, they said, 'That island was once a wicked dragon.' The children of the sea and the children of the land often went to the island, and there they had very happy times together."

This is the story that the mothers tell to their children when they look at the vases and see the picture of the goddess changing a dragon into an island. But when the children say, "Mother, where is the island? Cannot we go to it and play with the sea-children?" the mother answers, "Oh, this was all a long, long time ago, and no one can tell now where the island was."

WHY THE WATER IN RIVERS IS NEVER STILL.

All kinds of strange things came to pass in the days of long ago, but perhaps the strangest of all was that the nurses who cared for little children were not women, but brooks and rivers. The children and the brooks ran about together, and the brooks and rivers never said, "It is time to go to bed," for they liked to play as well as the children, and perhaps a little better. Sometimes the brooks ran first and the children followed. Sometimes the children ran first and the brooks followed. Of course, if any animal came near that would hurt the children, the brook or river in whose care they were left flowed quickly around them, so that they stood on an island and were safe from all harm.

Two little boys lived in those days who were sons of the king. When the children were old enough to run about, the king called the rivers and brooks to come before him. They came gladly, for they felt sure that something pleasant would happen, and they waited so quietly that no one would have thought they were so full of frolic.

"I have called you," said the king, "to give you the care of my two little sons. They like so well to run about that one nurse will not be enough to care for them, and of course it will be pleasanter for them to have many playmates. So I felt that it would be better to ask every river and every brook to see that they are not hurt or lost."

"We shall have the king's sons for our playmates!" whispered the rivers. "Nothing so pleasant ever happened to us before."

But the king went on, "If you keep my boys safely and well, and follow them so closely that they are not lost, then I will give you whatever gift you wish; but if I find that you have forgotten them one moment and they are lost or hurt, then you will be punished as no river was ever punished before."

The rivers and even the most frolicsome little brooks were again quiet for a moment. Then they all cried together, "O king, we will be good. There were never better nurses than we will be to your sons."

At first all went well, and the playmates had the merriest times that could be thought of. Then came a day when the sunshine was very warm, but the boys ran faster and farther than boys had ever run in the world before, and even the brooks could not keep up with them. The rivers had never been weary before, but when this warm day came, one river after another had some reason for being quiet. One complained, "I have followed the boys farther than any other river." "Perhaps you have," said another, "but I have been up and down and round and round till I have forgotten how it seems to be quiet." Another declared, "I have run about long enough, and I shall run no more." A little brook said, "If I were a great river, perhaps I could run farther," and a great river replied, "If I were a little brook, of course I could run farther."

So they talked, and the day passed. Night came before they knew it, and they could not find the boys.

"Where are my sons?" cried the king.

"Indeed, we do not know," answered the brooks and rivers in great fear, and each one looked at the others.

"You have lost my children," said the king, "and if you do not find them, you shall be punished. Go and search for them."

"Please help us," the rivers begged of the trees and plants, and everything that had life began to search for the lost boys. "Perhaps they are under ground," thought the trees, and they sent their roots down into the earth. "Perhaps they are in the east," cried one animal, and he went to the east. "They may be on the mountain," said one plant, and so it climbed to the very top of the mountain. "They may be in the village," said another, and so that one crept up close to the homes of men.

Many years passed. The king was almost broken-hearted, but he knew it was of no use to search longer, so he called very sadly, "Search no longer. Let each plant and animal make its home where it is. The little plant that has crept up the mountain shall live on the mountain top, and the roots of the trees shall stay under ground. The rivers"--Then the king stopped, and the rivers trembled. They knew that they would be punished, but what would the punishment be? The king looked at them. "As for you, rivers and brooks," he declared, "it was your work to watch my boys. The plants and trees shall find rest and live happily in their homes, but you shall ever search for my lost boys, and you shall never have a home."

So from that day to this the rivers have gone on looking for the lost children. They never stop, and some of them are so troubled that they flow first one way and then the other.

HOW THE RAVEN HELPED MEN.

The raven and the eagle were cousins, and they were almost always friendly, but whenever they talked together about men, they quarreled.

"Men are lazy," declared the eagle. "There is no use in trying to help them. The more one does for them, the less they do for themselves."

"You fly so high," said the raven, "that you cannot see how hard men work. I think that we birds, who know so much more than they, ought to help them."

"They do not work," cried the eagle. "What have they to do, I should like to know? They walk about on the ground, and their food grows close by their nests. If they had to fly through the air as we do, and get their food wherever they could, they might talk about working hard."

"That is just why we ought to help them," replied the raven. "They cannot mount up into the air as we do. They cannot see anything very well unless it is near them, and if they had to run and catch their food, they would surely die of hunger. They are poor, weak creatures, and there is not a humming-bird that does not know many things that they never heard of."

"You are a poor, weak bird, if you think you can teach men. When they feel hunger, they will eat, and they do not know how to do anything else. Just look at them! They ought to be going to sleep, and they do not know enough to do even that."

"How can they know that it is night, when they have no sun and no moon to tell them when it is day and when it is night?"

"They would not go to sleep even if they had two moons," said the eagle; "and you are no true cousin of mine if you do not let them alone."

So the two birds quarreled. Almost every time they met, they quarreled about men, and at last, whenever the eagle began to mount into the air, the raven went near the earth.

Now the eagle had a pretty daughter. She and the raven were good friends, and they never quarreled about men. One day the pretty daughter said, "Cousin Raven, are you too weak to fly as high as you used to do?"

"I never was less weak," declared the raven.

"Almost every day you keep on the ground. Can you not mount into the air?"

"Of course I can," answered the raven.

"There are some strange things in my father's lodge," said the pretty daughter, "and I do not know what they are. They are not good to eat, and I do not see what else they are good for. Will you come and see them?"

"I will go wherever you ask me," declared the raven.

The eagle's lodge was far up on the top of a high mountain, but the two birds were soon there, and the pretty daughter showed the raven the strange things.

He knew what they were, and he said to himself, "Men shall have them, and by and by they will be no less wise than the birds." Then he asked, "Has your father a magic cloak?"

"Yes," answered the pretty daughter.

"May I put it on?"

"Yes, surely."

When the raven had once put on the magic cloak, he seized the strange things and put them under it. Then he called, "I will come again soon, my pretty little cousin, and tell you all about the people on the earth."

The things under his cloak were strange indeed, for one was the sun, and one was the moon. There were hundreds of bright stars, and there were brooks and rivers and waterfalls. Best of all, there was the precious gift of fire. The raven put the sun high up in the heavens, and fastened the moon and stars in their places. He let the brooks run down the sides of the mountains, and he hid the fire away in the rocks.

After a while men found all these precious gifts. They knew when it was night and when it was day, and they learned how to use fire. They cannot mount into the air like the eagle, but in some things they are almost as wise as the birds.

THE STORY OF THE EARTH AND THE SKY.

The sky used to be very close to the earth, and of course the earth had no sunshine. Trees did not grow, flowers did not blossom, and water was not clear and bright. The earth did not know that there was any other way of living, and so she did not complain.

By and by the sky and the earth had a son who was called the Shining One.

When he was small, he had a dream, and he told it to the earth. "Mother Earth," he said, "I had a dream, and it was that the sky was far up above us. There was a bright light, and it made you more radiant than I ever saw you. What could the light have been?"

"I do not know, my Shining One," she answered, "for there is nothing but the earth and the sky."

After a long, long time, the Shining One was fully grown. Then he said to the sky, "Father Sky, will you not go higher up, that there may be light and warmth on the earth?"

"There is no 'higher up,'" declared the sky. "There is only just here."

Then the Shining One raised the sky till he rested on the mountain peaks.

"Oh! oh!" cried the sky. "They hurt. The peaks are sharp and rough. You are an unkind, cruel son."

"In my dreams you were still higher up," replied the Shining One, and he raised the sky still higher.

"Oh! oh!" complained the sky, "I can hardly see the peaks. I will stay on the rough rocks."

"You were far above the rocks in my dream," replied the Shining One.

Then when the sky was raised far above the earth and no longer touched even the peaks, a great change came over the earth. She, too, had thought the Shining One unkind, and she had said, "Shining One, it was only a dream. Why should you change the sky and the earth? Why not let them stay as they were before you had the dream?"

"O Mother Earth," he said, "I wish you could see the radiant change that has come to pass. The air is full of light and warmth and fragrance. You yourself are more beautiful than you were even in my dream. Listen and hear the song of the birds. See the flowers blossoming in every field, and even covering the rough peaks of the mountains. Should you be glad if I had let all things stay as they were? Was I unkind to make you so much more lovely than you were?"

Before the earth could answer, the sky began to complain. "You have spread over earth a new cloak of green, and of course she is beautiful with all her flowers and birds, but here am I, raised far above the mountain peaks. I have no cloak, nor have I flowers and birds. Shining One, give me a cloak."

"That will I do, and most gladly," replied the Shining One, and he spread a soft cloak of dark blue over the sky, and in it many a star sparkled and twinkled.

"That is very well in the night," said the heavens, "but it is not good in the daytime, it is too gloomy. Give me another cloak for the day." Then the Shining One spread a light blue cloak over the sky for the daytime, and at last the sky was as beautiful as the earth.

Now both sky and earth were contented. "I did not know that the earth was so radiant," said the sky. "I did not know that the sky was so beautiful," said the earth. "I will send a message to tell her how lovely she is," thought the sky, and he dropped down a gentle little rain.

"I, too, will send a message," thought the earth, "and the clouds shall carry it for me." That is why there is often a light cloud rising from the earth in the morning. It is carrying a good-morning message from the beautiful earth to the sky.

HOW SUMMER CAME TO THE EARTH.

PART I.

There was once a boy on the earth who was old enough to have a bow and arrows, but who had never seen a summer. He had no idea how it would look to have leaves on the trees, for he had never seen any such things. As for the songs of birds, he may have heard them in his dreams, but he never heard them when he was not asleep. If any one had asked, "Do you not like to walk on the soft grass?" he would have answered, "What is grass? I never saw any."

The reason why this boy had never heard of summer was because there had never been a summer on the earth. Far to the north the earth was covered with thick ice, and even farther south, where the boy lived, the ground was rarely free from ice and snow.

The boy's father was called the fisher. He taught his little son to hunt, and made him a bow like his own, only smaller. The boy was proud of his arrows, and was always happy when he went out to hunt. He had often shot a lynx, and once or twice he had shot a wolverine. Sometimes it chanced that he found nothing to shoot, and then he was not happy, for he realized how cold it was. His fingers ached, and his feet ached, and the end of his nose ached. "Oh, if I could only carry the wigwam fire about with me!" he cried, for he had no idea of any other warmth than that which came from the fire.

Now it chanced that Adjidaumo, the squirrel, was on a tree over the boy's head, and he heard this cry. He dropped a piece of ice upon the end of the boy's little red nose, and the boy bent his bow. Then he realized who it was, and he cried, "O Adjidaumo, you are warm. You have no fingers to ache with the cold. I am warm just twice a day, once in the morning and once at night."

"Boys do not know much," replied Adjidaumo, dancing lightly on the topmost bough. "The end of my nose is warm, and I have no fingers like yours to be cold, but if I had chanced to have any, I have an idea that would have kept them warm."

"What is an idea?" asked the boy.

"An idea is something that is better than a fire," replied the squirrel, "for you can carry an idea about with you, and you have to leave the fire at home. A lynx has an idea sometimes, and a wolverine has one sometimes, but a squirrel has one twice as often as a boy."

The poor boy was too cold to be angry, and he begged, "Adjidaumo, if there is any way for me to keep warm, will you not tell me what it is? A lynx would be more kind to me than you are, and I am sure a wolverine would tell me."

Adjidaumo had rarely been cold, but when he realized how cold the boy was, he was sorry for him, and he said, "All you have to do is to go home and cry. When your father says, 'Why do you cry?' answer nothing but 'Boo-hoo, boo-hoo, boo-hoo! Get me summer, get me summer!'"

Now this boy rarely cried, but his hands and feet were so very cold that he thought he would do as the squirrel had told him, and he started for home. As soon as he reached the wigwam, he threw himself down upon the ground and cried. He cried so hard that his tears made a river that ran out of the wigwam door. It was a frozen river, of course, but when the fisher saw it, he knew it was made of the tears of his little son. "What are you crying for?" he asked, but all the boy answered was "Boo-hoo, boo-hoo! Get me summer, father, get me summer!"

"Summer," repeated the fisher thoughtfully. "It is not easy to get summer, but I will find it if I can."

PART II.

The fisher made a great feast for the animals that he thought could help him to find summer. The otter, the lynx, the badger, and the wolverine came. After they had eaten, the hunter told them what he wished to do, and they all set out to find summer.

For many days they traveled, and at last they came to a high mountain upon whose summit the sky seemed to rest.

"That is where summer is," declared the badger. "All we have to do is to climb to the summit and take it from the heavens." So they all climbed and climbed, till it seemed as if they would never reach the top. After a long time they were on the very highest summit, but the heavens were above them.

"We cannot reach it," said the fisher.

"Let us try," said the lynx.

"I will try first," said the otter. So the otter sprang up with all his might, but he could not touch the heavens. He rolled down the side of the mountain, and then he ran home. The badger tried, and the beaver tried, and the lynx tried, but not one of them could leap far enough to reach the heavens. "Now I will try," said the wolverine. "I am not going to climb away up here for nothing." The fisher watched most eagerly, for he thought, "There's my boy at home crying, and what shall I do if I cannot get the summer for him?"

The wolverine leaped farther than any wolverine ever leaped before, and he went where no animal on the earth had ever been before, for he went straight through the floor of the heavens. Of course the fisher followed, and there they were in a more lovely place than any one on the earth had ever dreamed of, for they were in the land of summer, and summer had never come to the earth.

The soft, warm air went down through the hole in the floor and spread over the earth. Birds flew down, singing happily as they flew, and all kinds of flowers that are on the earth to-day made their way through the hole as fast as they could, for they knew all about the little boy in the wigwam who was wishing that summer would come.

Now there were people in the heavens, and when they found that summer was going down to the earth through the hole in the floor, they cried out to the Great Spirit, "Take summer away from him, take it away from him!" and they shot their arrows at the fisher and the wolverine. The wolverine dropped through the hole, but the fisher was not quick enough, and he could not get away.

The Great Spirit said, "The heavens have the summer all the year, but the earth shall have summer half the year. I shall close the hole in the floor so the fisher cannot go down to earth again, but I will make him into a fish and give him a place in the heavens."

When the Indians look up at the sky, they see a fish in the stars, and they say, "That is the good fisher who gave us the beautiful summer."

THE STORY OF THE FIRST SNOWDROPS.

An old man sat alone in his house. It Was full of shadows; it was dark and gloomy. The old man cared nothing for the shadows or the darkness, for he was thinking of all the mighty deeds that he had done. "There is no one else in the world," he muttered, "who has done such deeds as I," and he counted them over aloud. A sound outside of the house interrupted him. "What can it be?" he said to himself. "How dares anything interrupt me? I have told all things to be still. It sounds like the rippling of waters, and I have told the waters to be quiet in their beds. There it is again. It is like the singing of birds, and I have sent the birds far away to the south."

Some one opened the door and came in. It was a youth with sunny curls and rosy face.

"Who said you might come in?" muttered the old man.

"Did not you?" asked the youth, with a merry little laugh. "I am really afraid that I came without asking. You see, every one is glad to see me and"--

"I am not," interrupted the old man.

"I have heard rumors of your great deeds," said the youth, "and I came to see whether the tales are true."

"The deeds are more true than the tales," muttered the old man, "for the tales are never great enough. No one can count the wonderful things I have done."

"And what are they?" asked the young man gravely, but with a merry little twinkle in his eyes that would have made one think of the waves sparkling in the sunlight. "Let us see whether you or I can tell the greatest tale."

"I can breathe upon a river and turn it to ice," said the old man.

"I can breathe upon the ice and turn it to a river," said the youth.

"I can say to water, 'Stand still,' and it will not dare to stir."

"I can say, 'Stand no longer,' and it will go running and chattering down the mountain side."

"I shake my white head," said the old man, "and snow covers the earth."

"I shake my curls," said the young man, "and the air sparkles with sunshine. In a moment the snow is gone."

"I say to the birds, 'Sing no more. Leave me,' and they spread their wings and fly far away."

"I say, 'Little birds, come back,' and in a moment they are back again and singing their sweetest songs to me."

"No one can count the leaves," said the old man, "but whether I shake the trees with my icy touch, or whether I turn my cold breath upon them, they fall to the ground with fear and trembling. Are there any rumors of my deeds as great as that?"

The young man answered gravely, but with a laugh in his voice, "I never saw any leaves falling to the ground, for when I appear, they are all fair and green and trembling with the gladness of my coming."

So the two talked all night long. As morning came near, the old man appeared weary, but the youth grew merrier. The sunlight brightened, and the youth turned to the open door. The trees were full of birds, and when they saw him, they sang, "O beautiful spring! glad are we to look again upon your face."

"My own dear birds!" cried spring. He turned to say good-by, but the old man was gone, and where he had stood were only snowflakes. But were they snowflakes? He looked again. They were little white snowdrops, the first flowers of spring, the only flowers that can remember the winter.

WHY THE FACE OF THE MOON IS WHITE.

An Indian chief had a fair young daughter. One day the wind came to him and said, "Great chief, I love your daughter, and she loves me. Will you give her to me to be my wife?"

"No," answered the chief.

The next day the maiden herself went to the chief and said, "Father, I love the wind. Will you let me go with him to his lodge and be his wife?"

"No," declared the chief, "I will not. When the wind was a child, he often came into my wigwam through some tiny hole, and try as I would to make my fire, he always put it out. He knows neither how to fight nor how to hunt, and you shall not be his wife."

Then the chief hid his daughter in a thick grove of dark spruces. "The wind might see her in a pine," he thought, "but he will never catch sight of her in a grove of spruces."

Now the wind could make himself invisible if he chose, and all the time that the chief was talking, the wind was close beside him listening to every word. When the next night came, the wind ran round and round the grove of spruces until he discovered a tiny place where he could get in. When he came out, the maiden was with him. He did not dare to go near the Indians to live, for he was afraid that the chief would come and take her away from him; so he built a new lodge far to the north-ward. To that lodge he carried the maiden, and she became his wife.

Neither the wind nor his young wife had thought that the chief could ever find them, but he searched and searched, and at last he came to their lodge. The wind hid his wife and made himself invisible, but the father struck all about with his great war-club, and a hard blow fell upon the head of the wind. He knew no more of what the chief was doing.

When he came to himself, he discovered that his wife was gone, and he set out in search of her. He roamed about wildly in the forest, and at last he saw her in a canoe with her father on the Big-Sea-Water. "Come with me," he called. She became as white as snow, but she could not see the wind, because after the blow upon his head he had forgotten how to make himself visible.

He was so angry with the chief that he blew with all his might upon the tiny canoe. "Let it tip over," he thought. "I can carry my wife safely to land." The canoe did tip over, and both the chief and his daughter fell into the water. "Come, dear wife," cried the wind. "Here is my hand." He did not remember that he was invisible, and that she could not see his hand. That is why she fell down, down, through the deep water to the bottom of the lake. The chief, too, lost his life, for the wind did not try to help him.

When the wind discovered that his wife was gone from him, he became almost wild with sorrow. "The wind never blew so sadly before," said the people in the wigwams.

The Great Spirit was sorry that the chief's daughter had fallen into the water and lost her life, and the next night he bore her up to the stars and gave her a home in the moon. There she lives again, but her face is white, as it was when she fell from the canoe. On moonlight nights she always looks down upon the earth, searching for the wind, for she does not know that he is invisible. The wind does not know that far away in the moon is the white face of his lost wife, and so he roams through the forest and wanders about the rocks and the mountains, but never thinks of looking up to the moon.

WHY ALL MEN LOVE THE MOON.

Thunder and Lightning were going to give a feast. It was to be a most delightful banquet, for all the good things that could be imagined were to be brought from every corner of the world.

For many days before the feast these good things were coming. The birds flew up with what they could find in the cold air of the north and the warm air of the south. The fishes came from the east and from the west with what they could find in the cold water or in the warm water. As for what grew on the earth, there was no end to the luxuries that came every morning and every evening. Squirrels brought nuts, crows brought corn, the ants brought sweet things of many kinds. Food that was rich and rare came from India and Japan. The butterflies and the humming-birds were to arrange the flowers, the peacocks and the orioles promised to help make the place beautiful, and the waves and the brooks agreed to make their most charming music.

Thunder and Lightning were talking about whom to invite, and they questioned whether to ask the sun, the moon, and the wind. These three were children of the star mother.

"The star mother has been so kind to us that I suppose we ought to invite her children," said Thunder.

"The moon is charming, but the sun and the wind are rough and wild. If I were the star mother, I would keep them in a corner all day, and they should stay there all night, too, if they did not promise to be gentle," said Lightning.

"We must invite them," replied Thunder, with what sounded much like a little growl, "but it would be delightful if they would agree to stay away, all but the moon."

That is why the sun and wind were invited as well as the moon. When the invitation came, the two brothers said to their little sister, "You are too small to go to a feast, but perhaps they asked you because they were going to ask us."

"Star mother, I think I will stay at home," said the moon tearfully.

"No, little moon," replied the star mother; "go to the feast with the other children."

So the three children went to the feast, and the star mother waited for them to come home.

When they came, she asked, "What did you bring for me?" The hands of the sun were full of good things, but he said, "I brought only what I am going to eat myself," and he sat down in a corner with his back to the others, and went on eating.

"Did you bring anything for me?" she asked the wind.

"I brought some good things halfway home, and then I was weary of carrying them," answered the wind, "so I have eaten them."

"I should never have imagined that you would be so selfish," said the star mother sadly, and she asked the little moon, "My daughter, did you bring anything for me?"

"Yes, star mother," answered the little moon, and she gave her mother more good things than any one had ever seen in their home before. There were rare luxuries that the fishes and the birds had brought. There were rich colors that the peacocks and orioles had promised, and there was even some of the charming music that the waves and brooks had agreed to make.

The star mother praised the little maiden. Then she looked at her two boys. She was sad, for she knew that they must be punished for their selfishness. "Sun," said she, "you wish to turn your back on all, and your punishment shall be that when the warm days of summer have come, all men will turn their backs on you." To the wind she said, "Wind, you thought of no one but yourself. When the storm is coming and you are afraid and fly before it, no one shall think of you. All men shall close their doors against you and fasten them." Then to her little daughter she said, "My little moon, you were unselfish and thoughtful. You shall always be bright and beautiful, and men shall love you and praise you whenever they look upon your gentle, kindly face."

This is why men hide from the sun and the wind, but never from the moon.

WHY THERE IS A HARE IN THE MOON.

Many strange things happened long ago, and one of them was that a hare, a monkey, and a fox agreed to live together. They talked about their plan a long time. Then the hare said, "I promise to help the monkey and the fox." The monkey declared, "I promise to help the fox and the hare." The fox said, "I promise to help the hare and the monkey." They shook hands, or rather shook paws. There was something else to which they agreed, and that was that they would kill no living creature.

The manito was much pleased when he heard of this plan, but he said to himself, "I should like to make sure that what I have heard is true, and that they are really gentle and kind to others as well as to themselves. I will go to the forest and see how they behave toward strangers."

The manito appeared before the three animals, but they thought he was a hunter. "May I come into your lodge and rest?" he asked. "I am very weary."

All three came toward him and gave him a welcome. "Come into our lodge," they said. "We have agreed to help one another, so we will help one another to help you."

"I have been hungry all day," said the manito, "but I should rather have such a welcome than food."

"But if you are hungry, you must have food," declared the three animals. "If there were anything in our lodge that you would care to eat, you might have part of it or all of it, but there is nothing here that you would like."

Then said the monkey, "I have a plan. I will go out into the forest and find you some food."

When the monkey came back, he said, "I found a tree with some fruit on it. I climbed it and shook it, and here is the fruit. There was only a little of it, for fruit was scarce."

"Will you not eat part of it yourself?" asked the manito.

"No," answered the monkey. "I had rather see you eat it, for I think you are more hungry than I."

The manito wished to know whether the fox and the hare would behave as unselfishly toward him, and he said, "My good friends, the fruit was indeed welcome, but I am still hungry."

Then the fox said, "I will go out into the forest and see what I can find for you."

When the fox came back, he said, "I shook the trees, but no more fruit fell. I could not climb the trees, for my paws are not made for climbing, but I searched on the ground, and at last I found some hominy that a traveler had left, and I have brought you that."

The manito had soon eaten the hominy. He wished to know whether the hare would behave as kindly as the others, and before long he said, "My good friends, the hominy was indeed welcome, but I am still hungry."

Then the hare said, "I will gladly go out into the forest and search for food." He was gone a long time, but when he came back, he brought no food.

"I am very hungry," said the manito.

"Stranger," said the hare, "if you will build a fire beside the rock, I can give you some food."

The manito built a fire, and the hare said, "Now I will spring from the top of the rock upon the fire. I have heard that men eat flesh, that is taken from the fire, and I will give you my own."

The hare sprang from the rock, but the manito caught him in his hands before the flame could touch him, and said, "Dear, unselfish little hare, the monkey and the fox have welcomed me and searched the forest through to find me food, but you have done more, for you have given me yourself. I will take the gift, little hare, and I will carry you in my arms up to the moon, so that every one on the earth may see you and hear the tale of your kindness and unselfishness."

The Indians can see a hare in the moon, and this is the story that they tell their children about it.

THE CHILDREN IN THE MOON.

They had no idea where they came from. All they knew was that they lived on the hill, and that the old man of the hill called them Jack and Jill. They had plenty of berries to eat, and when night came, they had soft beds of fir to sleep on. There were all kinds of animals on the hill, and they were friendly to the two children. They could have had a most delightful time playing all day long if it had not been for having to carry water.

Every morning, just as soon as the first rays of the sun could be seen from their home, they heard the voice of the old man of the hill calling, "Jack! Jill! Take your pail and get some water." Whenever they were having an especially pleasant game with some of the animals, they heard the same call, "Take your pail and get some water." It is no wonder that Jack awoke one night when no one called and said, "Jill, did he say we must get some water?" "I suppose so," answered Jill sleepily, and they went out with the pail.

The moon was shining down through the trees, and they imagined that she was nearer than ever before. The forest was not half so lonely with her gentle face looking down upon them. Soon they felt happier than at first, and they played little games together, running from tree to tree.

"We have spilled half the water," said Jill.

"There's plenty left," said Jack, "if half is spilled."

"Do you suppose there are any children who play games whenever they like and do not have to carry water?"

"Plenty of them," declared Jack.

"Jack and Jill Went up the hill To get a pail of water,"

sang a voice so clear that it seemed close at hand, and so soft that it seemed far away.

Jack started, fell, and rolled down the hillside, and Jill came tumbling after.

As for the water, what was left was spilled before Jack had rolled over once; and before he had rolled over twice, the same voice sang,--

"Jack fell down And broke his crown, And Jill came tumbling after."

"It is about us," cried Jill.

"I have not broken any crown," said Jack.

"It is the crown of your head," declared Jill.

"Oh!" said Jack; "but where's the water?"

"It has gone tumbling down the hill," answered the same voice.

"How can water go tumbling?" cried Jill. "We tumbled."

"Water tumbles too," replied the voice, "especially when it is frozen."

"Oh!" said Jack.

"Oh!" said Jill.

"The stream is frozen," called the voice.

"What stream?" asked the children together.

"The stream that goes down the hill," answered the voice. "Did you not know that you were bringing water to keep the stream full?"

"No, indeed," said the children.

"The old man of the hill is only a rock, and what you thought his voice was only the water flowing around it."

[Illustration]

"Oh!" cried Jack.

"Oh!" cried Jill.

"The stream is frozen," said the voice, "and the earth has a cloak of snow and ice."

"Who are you?" asked Jill shyly.

"Do you really not know? What a strange child you are! I am the moon, of course. Very pleasant people live with me, and I have come to invite you both to go home with me. Will you come?"

The children looked up through the trees, and there was the gentle face of the moon, looking more gentle and kind than ever. "Come," said she, and they went very willingly. They have lived in the moon many years, but they never again carried a pail of water for a stream. "That is the work of the clouds and the sun," says the moon.

WHY THERE IS A MAN IN THE MOON.

"Goodman," said the goodwife, "you must go out into the forest and gather sticks for the fire. To-morrow will be Sunday, and we have no wood to burn."

"Yes, goodwife," answered the goodman, "I will go to the forest."

He did go to the forest, but he sat on a mossy rock and fished till it was dark, and so he brought home no wood. "The goodwife shall not know it," he thought. "I will go to the forest to-morrow morning and gather sticks."

When morning came, he crept softly out of the house when it was hardly light, and went to the forest. Soon he had as many sticks as he could carry, and he was starting for home when a voice called sternly, "Put those sticks down." He looked to the right, to the left, before him, behind him, and over his head. There was no one to be seen.

"Put those sticks down," said the voice again.

"Please, I do not dare to put them down," replied the goodman, trembling with fear. "They are to burn, and my wife cannot cook the dinner without them."

"You will have no dinner to-day," said the voice.

"The goodwife will not know that I did not gather them last night, and she will let me have some dinner. I am almost sure she will," the goodman replied.

"You must not gather sticks to-day," said the voice more sternly than ever. "It is Sunday. Put them down."

"Indeed, Mr. Voice, I dare not," whispered the goodman; and afar off he thought he heard his wife calling, "Goodman, where are you? There is no wood to burn."

"Will you put them down, or will you carry them forever?" cried the voice angrily.

"Truly, I cannot put them down, for I dare not go home without them," answered the goodman, shaking with fear from head to foot. "The goodwife would not like it."

"Then carry them forever," said the voice. "You care not for Sunday, and you shall never have another Sunday."

The goodman could not tell how it came about, but he felt himself being lifted, up, up, up, sticks and all, till he was in the moon.

"Here you shall stay," said the voice sternly. "You will not keep Sunday, and here you need not. This is the moon, and so it is always the moon's day, or Monday, and Monday it shall be with you always. Whenever any one looks up at the moon, he will say, 'See the man with the sticks on his back. He was taken to the moon because he gathered wood on Sunday.'"

"Oh dear, oh dear," cried the goodman, "what will the goodwife say?"

THE TWIN STARS.

In front of the little house was a pine-tree, and every night at the time when the children went to bed, a bright star appeared over the top of the tree and looked in at the window. The children were brother and sister. They were twins, and so they always had each other to play with.

"Now go to sleep," the mother would say when she had kissed them good-night, but it was hard to go to sleep when such a beautiful, radiant thing was shining in at the window of the little house.

"What do you suppose is in the star?" asked the sister.

"I think there are daisies and honey and violets and butterflies and bluebirds," answered the brother.

"And I think there are roses and robins and berries and humming-birds," said the sister.

"There must be trees and grass too, and I am sure there are pearls and diamonds."

"I can almost see them now," declared the sister. "I wish we could really see them. To-morrow let us go and find the star."

When morning came, the star was gone, but they said, "It was just behind the pine-tree, and so it must be on the blue mountain." The blue mountain was a long way off, but it looked near, and the twins thought they could walk to it in an hour. All day long they walked. They went through the lonely woods, they crossed brooks, they climbed hills, and still they could not find the radiant star that had looked in at their window. The hour had come when their mother always put them to bed and kissed them and said good-night, but now they had no mother, no good-night kiss, and no bed. They were tired and sleepy. They heard strange sounds in the forest, and they were frightened. "I am so tired," the sister whispered. "I am afraid a bear will come. I wish we could see the star."

The sky had grown dark, and a star could be seen here and there, but it was not their star. They went on till they could go no farther. "We will lie down on the grass," said the brother, "and cover ourselves up with leaves, and go to sleep."

Tired as they were, they did not have time to go to sleep before they heard a bear calling "Ugh! Ugh!" in the woods. They sprang up and ran out of the woods, and just before they came to the bottom of the hill, they saw right in front of them a beautiful little lake. They were not frightened any more, for there in the water was something radiant and shining. "It is our own star," said they, "and it has come down to us." They never thought of looking up into the sky over their heads. It was enough for them that the star was in the water and so near them. But was it calling them? They thought so. "Come," cried the brother, "take my hand, and we will go to the star." Then the spirit of the skies lifted them up gently and carried them away on a beautiful cloud.

The father and mother sat alone in the little house one evening, looking sadly out of the window through which the twins had looked. "There is the star that they loved," the mother said. "I have often listened to them while they talked of it. It is rising over the pine-tree in front of the house." They sat and watched the star. It was brighter and more radiant than ever, and in it the father and mother saw the faces of their lost children. "Oh, take us too, good spirit of the skies!" they cried. The spirit heard them, and when the next evening came, close beside the star there was another star. In that were the father and mother, and at last they and the children were all very happy to be together again.

THE LANTERN AND THE FAN.

In a Japanese village there once lived a man who had two sons. When the sons were grown up, each brought home a wife from another village a long distance away. The father was greatly pleased with his two daughters-in-law, and for many months they all lived very happily together.

At last the two young wives asked to go home to visit their friends. Among the Japanese the sons and the sons' wives must always obey the father, so the two wives said, "Father-in-law, it is a long, long time since we have seen our friends. May we go to our old home and visit them?" The father-in-law answered, "No." After many months they asked again, and again he answered, "No." Once more they asked. The father-in-law thought, "They care nothing for me, or they would not wish to leave me, but I have a plan, and I can soon know whether they love their father-in-law or not." Then he said to the older of the two wives, "You may go if you wish, but you must never come back unless you bring me fire wrapped in paper." To the younger he said, "You may go if you wish, but you must never come back unless you bring me wind wrapped in paper." The father-in-law thought, "Now I shall find out. If they care for me, they will search the country through till they find paper that will hold fire and wind."

The two young wives were so glad to visit their old friends that for almost a month they forgot all about the gifts that they were to carry to their father-in-law. At last, when it was time to go home, they were greatly troubled about what they must carry with them, and they asked a wise man where to find the strange things. "Paper that will hold fire and wind!" he cried. "There is no such paper in Japan." The two women asked one wise man after another, and every one declared, "There is no such paper in Japan." What should they do? They feared they would never see their home again. They were so sad that they left their friends and wandered a long distance into the forest. Great tears fell from their eyes.

"I do not let people cry in my woods," said a voice. "My trees do not grow well in salt water."

The poor wives were so sorrowful that they forgot to be afraid, and the older one said, "Can we help crying? Unless I can carry to my father-in-law fire wrapped in paper, I can never go home." "And I," wailed the younger, "unless I can carry wind wrapped in paper, I can never go home. None of the wise men ever heard of such things. What shall we do?"

"It is easy enough to wrap fire in paper," answered the voice. "Here is a piece of paper. Now watch." They watched, and the strangest thing in all the world happened right before their eyes. There was no one to be seen, but a piece of paper appeared on the ground and folded itself into a Japanese lantern. "Now put a candle inside," said the voice, "and you have paper holding fire. What more could you ask?"

Then the older woman was happy, but the younger was still sad. She saw now that fire could be carried in paper, but surely no one could carry wind. "O dear voice," she cried, "can any one carry wind in paper?"

"That is much easier than to carry fire," replied the voice, "for wind does not burn holes. Watch."

They watched eagerly. Another piece of paper came all by itself and lay on the ground between them. There was a picture on it of a tree covered with white blossoms. Two women stood under the tree, gathering the blossoms.

"The two women are yourselves," said the voice, "and the blossoms are the gifts that the father-in-law will give you when you go home."

"But I cannot go home," the younger wailed, "for I cannot carry wind wrapped in paper."

"Here is the paper, and there is always plenty of wind. Why not take them?"

"Indeed, I do not know how," the younger woman answered sorrowfully.

"This way, of course," said the voice. Some long, light twigs flew to the paper. It folded itself, over, under, together. It opened and closed, and it waved itself before the tearful face of the younger woman. "Does not the wind come to your face?" asked the voice, "and is it not the fan that has brought it? The lantern carries fire wrapped in paper, and the fan carries wind wrapped in paper."

Then, indeed, the two young women were happy, and when they came to the home of their father-in-law, he was as glad as they. He gave them beautiful gifts of gold and silver, and he said, "No one ever had such marvels before as the lantern and the fan, but in my home there are two more precious things than these, and they are my two dear daughters."

###

www.ingramcontent.com/pod-product-compliance
Lightning Source LLC
Chambersburg PA
CBHW070119290526
45789CB00005B/2070